D1606522

THEY SAID *WHAT?*

THEY SAID
WHAT?

Astonishing Quotes on American
Power, Democracy, and Dissent

JIM HUNT

PoliPointPress

They Said What? *Astonishing Quotes on American Power, Democracy, and Dissent*

13 12 11 10 09   1 2 3 4 5

Production management: BookMatters
Book design: George Mattingly, BookMatters
Cover design: Chris Hall

Library of Congress Cataloging-in-Publication Data
Hunt, Jim.
    They said what? : astonishing quotes on American power, democracy, and dissent / Jim Hunt.
    p. cm.
ISBN 978-0-9817091-6-1
1. United States—Politics and government—Quotations, maxims, etc.
2. United States—Officials and employees—Quotations.
3. Quotations, American.
I. Title.
JK31.H88   2009
081—dc22   2009023037

Published by:
PoliPointPress, LLC
80 Liberty Ship Way, Suite 22
Sausalito, CA 94965
(415) 339-4100

www.p3books.com
Distributed by Ingram Publisher Services
Printed in the USA

To Kim and Robin—

thanks for the memories.

Contents

Preface

During my three decades of teaching high school history and government, I found that textbooks tend to omit anything that could reflect poorly on American leaders or our national character. In effect, we've made a collective decision to turn these leaders into upright heroes without fault or guile.

Young people need role models, but it's also vitally important for them (and indeed for all of us) to see that the American experience is much more than virtue on parade. As W.E.B. Du Bois once said, "One is astonished in the study of history at the recurrence of the idea that evil must be forgotten, distorted, or skimmed over. . . . The difficulty, of course, with this philosophy is that history loses its value as an incentive and example; it paints perfect men and noble nations, but it does not tell the truth."

With that in mind, I began supplementing the standard textbooks with outside readings. I've always been fascinated by the history of our government's secret activities, including U.S. interventions in Central America, covert CIA operations, the FBI's COINTELPRO program, and the secret side of the atomic testing in the 1950s. As a teacher and a citizen, I thought that *every* American ought to know about these activities.

Eventually I began to collect documented quotes from famous leaders and personalities. Often my reaction as I read them was astonishment: "They said *what?*" When I shared the quotes with friends and colleagues, they had the same reaction. After I retired from teaching, I decided to organize the quotes into various subject areas, such as comments about democracy, political dissent, conquest and empire, racial and ethnic equality, and so on. This book is the result.

You certainly won't find any of these quotes in high school textbooks. One of the quotes may explain why that is so. In June 1964, Judge Edward Ruzzo ruled on whether former President Warren G. Harding's love letters to a married woman should be published. In his final decision, which banned the publication of the letters, Judge Ruzzo wrote, "Anything damaging to the image of the American President should be suppressed to protect the younger generation."

As a history teacher, I had to ask: protect the younger generation from what? From the truth? Why wouldn't we want our children (or ourselves for that matter) to know what our leaders really felt, and thought, and said?

Part of growing up is realizing that leaders aren't perfect. Many of the men and women quoted in this book did great things during their lives, but they were flawed and conflicted, as are we all. There's no real harm in recognizing this; in fact, it can be liberating. Their unvarnished words can give us real insight into our history, into what our leaders were really like and what they were really thinking, instead of the spin we get from textbooks and the media.

Sometimes we don't even get spin, as when government officials tell us explicitly that we have no right to know the truth. Another quote in the book, this one from an official with the U.S. Department of Defense, put it this way: "Look, if you think any American official is going to tell you the truth, then you're stupid."

Some of these quotes are shocking, some are almost unbelievable, and some are even fun. Some will give you pause to reflect on what you learned in school about the leaders who made these statements. They don't necessarily represent the "true America," but they do reveal a piece of our history that is all too often overlooked or left out.

I hope that history buffs and general readers alike will enjoy these quotes, but I especially hope that teachers will find this book a helpful supplement to their everyday curriculum. My experience in sharing these quotes with my young students has been incredibly positive over the years. Initially they were shocked and dismayed, as I was when first exposed to this material. But they also enjoyed hearing them or reading them, and in the end, they thanked me for giving them a new perspective on our history and its leaders. If we truly want students to take an interest in U.S. history, we should tell them the truth.

Power and Democracy

"The people who own the country ought to govern it."

—John Jay, first Chief Justice of the U.S. Supreme Court, 1795.

"A representative of the people is appointed to think for and not with his constituents."

—George Clymer of Pennsylvania, one of the "Founding Fathers," 1787.

"We have probably had too good an opinion of human nature in forming our confederation. Experience has taught us that men will not adopt and carry into execution the measures best calculated for their own good, without the intervention of a coercive power."

—George Washington, 1789.

"Men in general who are wholly destitute of property, are also too little acquainted with public affairs to form a right judgment, and too dependent on other men to have a will of their own."

—John Adams, 1790.

"All communities divide themselves into the few and the many. The first are the rich and well born, the other the mass of the people. The voice of the people has been said to be the voice of God; it is not true in fact. The people are turbulent and changing; they seldom judge or determine right. Give therefore to the first class a distinct, permanent share in the government. They will check the unsteadiness of the second. . . . Can a democratic assembly who annually revolve in the mass of the people, be supposed steadily to pursue the public good? Nothing but a permanent body can check the imprudence of democracy."

—Alexander Hamilton, 1791.

"Self-government! Why, these people are no more ready for self-government than gunpowder is for hell."

—General William Shafter, to a reporter who asked him if he thought the Cuban people would be successful in setting up their own government after the Spanish-American War, 1898.

"Further comment on the fairness of the elections is hardly necessary."

—Charles B. Curtis, U.S. Ambassador to the Dominican Republic, commenting on the 1930 Dominican Presidential elections in which U.S.-supported dictator Rafael Trujillo had garnered a total of 223,851 votes—more than the number of eligible voters in the country.

"The President ought to be allowed to hang two men every year without giving any reason or explanation."

—President Herbert Hoover, 1930.

"If you destroy the leisure class, you destroy civilization. The leisure class can be defined by people who can afford to hire a maid."

—J. Pierpont Morgan, testifying at congressional hearings on higher taxes on the wealthy, February 1936.

"The United States is making it crystal clear that it will use force if necessary to prevent Italy from going communist in its upcoming elections."

—U.S. State Department spokesman Richard Browning, March 1948. In 1948 polls in Italy were showing that in the upcoming election, the Communist and Socialist Parties were going to win a majority in the Italian government. As a result, the CIA spent $20 million to guarantee that didn't happen.

"We should do what is necessary even if the result is to change the American way of life. We could lick the whole world if we are willing to adopt the system of Adolph Hitler."

—Joint Chiefs of Staff report to President Dwight D. Eisenhower, August 1953.

"I don't believe Diem wants to hold elections and I believe we should support him in this."

—Secretary of State John Foster Dulles, to an aide, regarding the 1954 Geneva Convention's plan for the Vietnamese people to elect their own government in 1956. Ngo Dinh Diem, who the United States had installed as President of South Vietnam in 1954, and Dulles both knew that if elections were held, the people of Vietnam would have elected the North Vietnamese communist leader Ho Chi Minh by a landslide.

"He had his torture chambers, he had his political assassinations. But he kept law and order, cleaned the place up, made it sanitary, built public works, and he didn't bother the United States. So that was fine with us."

—U.S. Consul General Henry Dearborn, ranking American diplomat in the Dominican Republic in 1961. Dearborn was referring to Generalissimo Rafael Trujillo, who brutally ruled the Dominican Republic for 30 years.

"Listen to me, Mr. Ambassador. Fuck your Parliament and your constitution! America is an elephant. Cyprus is a flea. Greece is a flea. If these two fleas continue itching the elephant, they may just get whacked by the elephant's trunk, whacked good. . . . We pay a lot of good American dollars to the Greeks, Mr. Ambassador. If your Prime Minister gives me talk about democracy, Parliament, and constitutions, he, his Parliament, and his constitution may not last very long."

—President Lyndon B. Johnson, during an oval office conversation with the Greek ambassador, 1967. The ambassador was meeting with Johnson to protest U.S. interference in Greek affairs.

"Latin American military juntas were good for the United States. They were the only force capable of controlling political crises. Law and order were better than the messy struggle for democracy and freedom."

—Richard Helms, CIA Director, in a memorandum entitled "The Political Role of the Military in Latin America," April 30, 1968.

"This country is going so far to the right you are not even going to recognize it."

—U.S. Attorney General John Mitchell, 1970.

"Not a nut or bolt will be allowed to reach Chile under Allende. Once Allende comes to power we will do all within our power to condemn Chile and Chileans to utmost deprivation and poverty."

—U.S. Ambassador to Chile, Edward Korry, during the Chilean elections of 1970.

"It's that son of a bitch Allende. We're going to smash him!"

—President Richard M. Nixon, October 1970.

"The issues are much too important for the Chilean voters to be left to decide for themselves."

—Secretary of State Henry Kissinger, in testimony to Congress regarding U.S. involvement in the overthrow of the Chilean government, 1973.

"It is quite obvious that there are inherently governmental actions which, if undertaken by the sovereign in protection of the interest of the nation's security, are lawful, but which if undertaken by private persons are not."

—President Richard M. Nixon, 1973.

"The architects of power in the United States must create a force that can be felt but not seen. Power remains strong when it remains in the dark; exposed to the sunlight it begins to evaporate."

—Samuel Huntington, Harvard political scientist, in his text, *American Politics*, 1981.

"We stand with you, sir. . . . We love your adherence to democratic principle and to the democratic process."

—Vice President George H. W. Bush, praising Ferdinand Marcos, right-wing dictator of the Philippines, 1981.

"You have the freedom here to do what you want to do with your money, and to me, that is worth all the political freedom in the world."

—Douglas McDermott, a U.S. banker in Venezuela, commenting on the murderous government of the U.S.-supported dictator Pérez Jiménez, 1985.

"One of the awkward questions we faced was whether to reconstitute Congress after a nuclear attack. It was decided that no, it would be easier to operate without them."

—James Mann, a writer at the Center for Strategic and International Studies, speaking about a highly classified program during the 1980s in which Dick Cheney, Donald Rumsfeld, and a group of other Reagan administration officials simulated nuclear attacks during which they would be flown or driven to top-secret bunkers for three to four days at a time, pretending a nuclear catastrophe with the Soviets had occurred. Rather than follow federal law and the Constitution, they planned a different future for the United States. The simulations did not involve Congress and, in fact, the legislative branch was not even told of the exercises.

"Negotiations are a euphemism for capitulation if the shadow of power is not cast across the bargaining table."

—Secretary of State George Schultz, 1986.

"Democracy used to be a good thing, but now it has gotten into the wrong hands."

—Senator Jesse Helms of North Carolina, 1988.

"What right does Congress have to go around making laws just because they deem it necessary?"

—Marion Barry, mayor of Washington, D.C., 1988

"There ought to be limits to freedom."

—George W. Bush, governor of Texas, after unsuccessfully filing a lawsuit to shut down a political parody site, www.georgewbush.com, 1996.

"Customary international law cannot bind the executive branch under the Constitution because it is not federal law."

—John Yoo, deputy assistant attorney general in the Office of Legal Counsel of the U.S. Department of Justice, and Robert Delahunty, Justice Department Counsel, in a memo, January 9, 2002.

"I'm with the Bush-Cheney team, and I'm here to stop the count."

—John Bolton, speaking to election workers who were busy counting ballots for Miami-Dade County, Florida, in the 2000 presidential election.

"I fixed the election in Florida for George Bush."

—James Baker III, the Bush family lawyer, speaking to an audience of Russian oil industry oligarchs, March 2001.

"I want to thank all my citizens for coming."

—President George W. Bush, to a South Dakota audience, September 2002.

"We have put together a lethal military and we will kick his ass. . . . This is going to change. You watch—public opinion will change. We lead our publics. We cannot follow our publics."

—President George W. Bush, to Italian Prime Minister Silvio Berlusconi, when he tried to persuade Bush not to invade Iraq, January 2003.

"I am the ultimate decision-maker for this country."

—President George W. Bush, April 2003.

"[They're] a bunch of annoying gnats."

—Vice President Dick Cheney, referring to members of Congress, May 2003.

"I am fully committed to helping Ohio deliver its electoral votes to the president next year."

—Walter O'Dell, CEO of Diebold Elections Systems, a firm that makes electronic voting machines, in a fund-raising letter dated August 14, 2003. At the time of the 2004 election, Kenneth Blackwell, Ohio's Secretary of State, as well as the cochair of the Ohio Committee to Reelect George Bush, oversaw the administering of the 2004 presidential elections in Ohio. By the time of the election, he had managed to ensure that Diebold ran the voting machines in 40 percent of the state's counties.

"It would begin to unravel the fabric of our Constitution, and under those circumstances I would be open to the idea that the Constitution could be scrapped in favor of a military form of government."

—General Tommy Franks, commander of the U.S. assault on Baghdad, when asked what he thought another terrorist attack on the United States might mean for our government, November 21, 2003.

"I'm the commander—see, I don't need to explain—I don't need to explain why I say things. That's the interesting thing about being president."

—President George W. Bush, March 2004.

"As a leader, you can never admit a mistake."

—President George W. Bush, October 2004.

"Yes, I am. I change constitutions. I put churches in schools."

—Karl Rove, to his guide at the dedication of the William J. Clinton Library in November 2004. The guide had just said to Rove, "You're not such a scary guy."

Political Dissent

"The Bureau appreciates that the situation in Puerto Rico is unique because of conditions in Cuba, its accessibility to Puerto Rico, and the seemingly unrestricted travel of some of your citizens to Cuba. . . . *Bulet* [Bulletin] August 4, 1960, advised that a more positive effort must be made not only to curtail but to disrupt the activities of Puerto Rican nationalists."

—Memo from FBI Director J. Edgar Hoover to the FBI's San Juan, Puerto Rico headquarters, August 1960.

"There's nothing wrong with this country that we couldn't cure by turning it over to the police for a couple of weeks."

—George Wallace, Governor of Alabama, regarding the civil rights movement, 1964.

"Negro youth and moderates must be made to understand that if they succumb to revolutionary teaching, they will be dead revolutionaries."

—FBI document of the late 1960s.

"Those little shits on the campuses."

—President Lyndon B. Johnson, May 1967, talking to an aide about student protests against the war in Vietnam.

"When you see an epidemic like this cropping up all over the country—the same kind of people saying the same kind of things—you begin to get the picture that it is a national subversive activity.... All of these student protesters should be rounded up and put in a detention camp."

—Richard G. Kleindienst, Deputy Attorney General in the Nixon administration, 1969.

"Withdrawal of U.S. troops will become like salted peanuts to the American public: the more U.S. troops come home, the more will be demanded."

—National Security Advisor Henry Kissinger, in a memo to President Richard Nixon urging him to not begin removing troops from Vietnam, 1969.

"We must look to the university that receives our children. Is it prepared to deal with the challenge of the non-democratic left? One modest suggestion for my friends in the academic community: the next time a mob of students, waving their non-negotiable demands, starts pitching bricks and rocks at the Student Union—just imagine they are wearing brown shirts or white sheets and act accordingly."

—Vice President Spiro Agnew, 1970.

"They're [the students at Kent State] worse than the brown shirts and the communist element and also the night riders and the vigilantes. They're the worst type of people that we harbor in America. I think that we're up against the strongest, well-trained, militant revolutionary group that has ever assembled in America. . . . We are going to eradicate the problem, we're not going to treat the symptoms."

—James A. Rhodes, Governor of Ohio, in a speech given two days before the killing of students at Kent State University, May 1970.

"If it takes a bloodbath, then let's get it over with."

—California Governor Ronald Reagan, on how to handle student protests, May 5, 1970, the day following the killing of students at Kent State University.

"[The National Guard] should have shot all the trouble-makers."

—Seabury Ford, one of three special prosecutors in charge of presenting evidence to the Ohio grand jury following the killings of students at Kent State University, May 1970.

"No one from A.P. on social list for 3 mos." "No one, *Time, Newsweek, Post, Times.*" "Shaft . . . one by one." "Chop their heads—screw them."

—Notes by H.R. "Bob" Haldeman, White House chief of staff, written during an Oval Office meeting with President Richard M. Nixon, May 31, 1970.

Nixon: "They've got guys who'll go in and knock their heads off."

Haldeman: "Sure, murderers, guys that really, you know, that's what they really do. It's the regular strike buster types and . . . they're gonna beat the shit out of some of these people. And, uh, and hope they really hurt 'em. You know, I mean go in and smash some noses."

—Conversation between President Richard M. Nixon and White House Chief of Staff H. R. Haldeman, May 5, 1971. Haldeman had just suggested to Nixon that Teamsters' union "thugs" could be paid to assault groups of antiwar demonstrators.

"Anyone who opposes us, we'll destroy. As a matter of fact, anyone who doesn't support us, we'll destroy."

—Egil Krogh, aid to Domestic Chair John Erlichman, in the Nixon White House, 1972.

"We are America. Those other people are not."

—Rich Bond, chairman of the Republican National Committee, referring to protestors at the Republican National Convention, 1992.

"Never forget. The press is the enemy. The establishment is the enemy. The professors are the enemy. Professors are the enemy. Write that on the blackboard 100 times and never forget it."

—President Richard M. Nixon, speaking to National Security Advisor Henry Kissinger about criticism of his policies regarding Vietnam, December 14, 1972.

"We will not hesitate to discredit you."

—Vice President Dick Cheney to Hans Blix. Blix, former head of the United Nations' team to monitor Iraq's weapons of mass destruction, had refused to retract his statements contradicting the Bush administration's claims that Iraq possessed WMDs, 2002.

"It's beyond me how anybody can look at these protestors and call them anything other than what they are: anti-American, anticapitalist, pro-Marxist communists."

—Rush Limbaugh, February 2003.

"Once the war against Saddam begins, we expect every American to support our military, and if they can't do that, to shut up."

—Fox newsman Bill O'Reilly, April 2003.

"It's too bad Timothy McVeigh didn't go to the *New York Times* building."

—Anne Coulter, April, 2003

"Americans who didn't vote for Bush are traitors."

—Anne Coulter, October, 2004.

"Go fuck yourself."

—Vice President Dick Cheney, November 2006, in response to a question from Senator Patrick Leahy of Vermont regarding Cheney's possible involvement in aiding the Halliburton Corporation to gain government contracts.

Conquest, Manifest Destiny, and Empire

"They were well built, with good bodies and handsome features. . . . They do not bear arms and do not know of them for I showed them a sword and they took it by the edge and cut themselves out of ignorance. They have no iron, their spears are made of cane. . . . They would make fine servants. . . . With 50 men we could subjugate them all and make them do whatever we want."

—Christopher Columbus, in his log, October 1492.

"A hundred *castellanoes* are as easily obtained for a woman as for a farm, and it is very general and there are plenty of dealers who go about looking for girls; those from nine to ten are now in demand."

—Christopher Columbus, in a letter to a friend in 1500. Columbus knew of and condoned the sex-slave trade in the Caribbean which began in 1493.

"The soldiers mowed down dozens with point-blank volleys, loosed the dogs to rip open limbs and bellies, chased fleeing Indians into the bush to skewer them on sword and pike, and with God's aid soon gained a complete victory, killing many Indians and capturing others who were also then killed."

—Ferdinand Columbus, in his biography of his father, c. 1512.

"The manner of how to suppress them [the Native Americans] is so often related and approved, I omit it here: and you have 20 examples of how the Spaniards got the West Indies and forced the treacherous and rebellious infidels to do all manner of drudgery work and slavery for them."

—Captain John Smith, using Columbus's treatment of Indians as a model for his "get tough" policy regarding Indians in Virginia, 1624.

"God ended the controversy by sending the smallpox amongst the Indians."

—Increase Mather, Puritan minister, 1631.

"But for the natives in these parts, God hath so pursued them, as for 300 miles space the greatest part of them are swept away by the smallpox which still continues among them. So, as God hath thereby cleared our title to this place, those who remain in these parts, being in all not 50, have put themselves under our protection."

—John Winthrop, governor of Massachusetts Bay Colony, regarding the devastation of Indians by raging smallpox epidemics, 1634.

"Those that escaped the fire were slain with the sword; some hewed to pieces, others run through with their rapiers so they were quickly dispatched, and very few escaped. It was conceived they thus destroyed about 400 at this time. It was a fearful sight to see them thus frying in the fire and streams of blood quenching the same, and horrible was the stink thereof, but the victory seemed a sweet sacrifice and they gave prayers therefore to God, who had wrought so wonderfully for them, thus to enclose their enemies in their hands and give them so speedy a victory over so proud and insulting an enemy."

—William Bradford, Massachusetts Bay Colony, writing of a massacre of a village of Pequot Indians in his *History of the Plymouth Plantation*, 1636.

"We shot them like dogs."

—Davy Crockett, September 1813, reporting on Andrew Jackson's militiamen from Tennessee and Georgia slaughtering over 500 Creek Indians at Taladega and Talluschatches, Georgia.

"Yes: Mexico must be thoroughly chastised. The time has come for the world to realize that America knows how to crush as well as how to expand."

—Poet Walt Whitman, as editor of the *Brooklyn Eagle*, 1846.

"We must renounce the barbarous tyranny and superstitions of Mexico. It would be folly to tolerate the establishment of this ignorant and fanatical colored population on the borders of the United States."

—U.S. Secretary of the Treasury Robert J. Walker, 1846.

"If they—the Indians—stand up against the progress of civilization and industry, they must be relentlessly crushed. The westward course of population is neither to be denied nor delayed for the sake of all the Indians that ever called this country their home. They must yield or perish."

—Report of the Commissioner of Indian Affairs, 1873.

"Mexico must be made to *feel* this war. It would almost seem that they, like the Israelites of old, had brought upon themselves *the vengeance of the Almighty,* and we ourselves *had been raised up to overthrow* and UTTERLY DESTROY THEM *as a separate and distinct nation.*"

—*New York Globe* editorial, October 19, 1847.

"It is our destiny to have Cuba and it is folly to debate the question. It naturally belongs to the American continent."

—Senator Stephen A. Douglas, 1898.

"The Pacific Ocean is ours."

"God has marked the American people as his chosen nation to finally lead the regeneration of the world. This is the divine mission of America, and it holds for us all the profit, all the glory, all the happiness possible to man. We are trustees of the world's progress, guardians of its righteous peace."

"God has not been preparing the English-speaking and Teutonic peoples for a thousand years for nothing. . . . He has given us the spirit of progress to overwhelm the forces of reaction throughout the earth. He has made us adept in government that we may administer government among savages and senile people. . . . And of all our race He has marked the American people as His chosen nation to finally lead in the redemption of the world."

—Senator Albert Beveridge of Indiana, 1900–1901.

"America would never act unjustly or wrongly. Hence, whatever position America takes is right and whoever opposes American expansion is morally derelict."

—President Theodore Roosevelt, 1902.

"But, unfortunately [the Philippine Islands] are infested by Filipinos. There are millions of them there, and it is to be feared that their extinction will be slow. Let's all be frank, WE DO NOT WANT THE FILIPINOS, WE WANT THE PHILIPPINES."

—Editorial in the San Francisco *Argonaut*, 1902.

"The whole hemisphere will be ours in fact, as, by virtue of our superiority of race, it already is ours morally."

—President William H. Taft, 1912.

"I spent 33 years in active service as a member of the [U.S.] Marine Corps. And during that period I spent most of my time being a high-class muscleman for Big Business, for Wall Street and the bankers. In short, I was a racketeer for capitalism. Thus I helped make Mexico safe for American oil interests in 1914. I helped make Haiti and Cuba a decent place for the National City Bank to collect revenues in. I helped purify Nicaragua for the international banking house of Brown Brothers in 1900–1912. I brought light to the Dominican Republic for American sugar interests in 1916. I helped make Honduras 'right' for American fruit companies in 1903. . . . I had a swell racket. . . . I might have given Al Capone a few hints. The best he could do was operate in three cities. The Marines operated on three continents. . . .

"If only more of today's military personnel would realize that they are being used by the owning elites as a publicly subsidized capitalist goon squad."

—U.S. Marine General Smedley D. Butler, who headed many of the U.S. interventions in Latin America in the early 1900s.

"Since trade ignores national boundaries and the manufacturer plans on having the world as a market, the flag of this nation must follow, and the doors of the nations which are closed against him must be battered down. Concessions obtained by financiers must be safeguarded by ministers of state, even if the sovereignty of unwilling nations be outraged in the process. Colonies must be obtained or planted, in order that no useful corner of the world may be overlooked or left unused."

—President Woodrow Wilson, 1915.

"The United States considers its own interests. The integrity of other American nations is an incident, not an end."

—Secretary of State Robert Lansing, 1915.

"Practically indiscriminate killing of natives has gone on for some time. The most startling thing of its kind that has ever taken place in the Marine Corps."

—U.S. Marine General George Barnett, October 14, 1920, regarding the U.S. occupation of Haiti.

"We do control the destinies of Central America and we do so for the simple reason that the national interest absolutely dictates such a course. . . . Until now Central America has always understood that governments which we recognize and support stay in power, while those we do not recognize and support fail."

—Excerpt from a 1927 U.S. State Department memorandum by Undersecretary of State Robert Olds.

"We have about 50 percent of the world's wealth, but only 6.3 percent of its population. . . . In this situation, we cannot fail to be the object of envy and resentment. Our real task in the coming period is to devise a pattern of relationships, which will permit us to maintain this position of disparity. . . . [W]e will have to dispense with all sentimentality and daydreaming. . . . We should cease to talk about vague and unreal objectives such as human rights, the raising of the living standard, and democratization. The day is not far off when we are going to have to deal in straight power concepts. The less we are then hampered by idealistic slogans, the better."

—U.S. State Department Policy Planning Study (#23), 1948.

"The United States and other free nations will, within a period of a few years at most, experience a decline in economic activity of serious proportions unless more positive government programs are developed. . . . Each part in the neat structure of the global political economy reinforces the whole; constant global military mobilization [will] stimulate the U.S. economy, lubricate global trade, bind the other capitalist powers to the U.S. in a subsidiary role, fuel the ideological crackdown on radical thought, and eventually destroy the Soviet Union."

—Excerpt from National Security Council Memorandum NSC-68, 1950.

"The United States should do everything in its power to alter or abolish any regime not openly allied with America."

—Secretary of State John Foster Dulles, June 1953.

"Underdeveloped countries with rich resources now have an object lesson in the heavy cost that must be paid by one of their number which goes berserk with fanatical nationalism. It is perhaps too much to hope that Iran's experience will prevent the rise of Mossadeghs in other countries, but that experience may at least strengthen the hands of more reasonable and more far-reaching leaders."

—Editorial comments in the *New York Times*, August 6, 1954, after the CIA had instigated the overthrow of the government of Iran. The Eisenhower administration had decided that democratically elected Iranian Premier Mohammed Mossadegh had to be forcibly removed from power when he announced that he was nationalizing all of the oil fields in Iran.

"I don't feel we did wrong in taking this great country away from [the Indians]. . . . There were great numbers of people who needed new land, and the Indians were self-ishly trying to keep it for themselves."

—John Wayne, 1971.

"Puerto Rico became a part of the United States by an act of conquest, [and] even if the people were to vote for inde-pendence, Puerto Rico can't become so . . . neither inde-pendence, developed commonwealth, or statehood can be had. Puerto Rico must remain a colony."

—Senator Henry Jackson, 1974.

"We must decide now whether we intend to remain the strongest nation in the world, or whether we must accept now that we will let ourselves slip into inferiority, into a position of weakness in a harsh world where principles unsupported by power are victimized, and that we will become a nation with more of a past than a future."

—Secretary of Defense Harold Brown, in support of the argument that the United States should forcefully overturn the overthrow of the unpopular, dictatorial regime of Park Chung Hee in South Korea, 1979.

"Our first objective is to prevent the reemergence of a new rival. We must maintain the mechanisms for deterring potential competitors from even aspiring to a larger or global role."

—Excerpt from a Defense Department planning paper, 1992.

"Iraq was a natural ally of moderate Arab states. The fact that Saddam was a murderous thug did not change this."

—Peter Rodman, former Reagan-Bush National Security Council executive, 1992.

"We are on the verge of global transformation. All we need is the right major crisis and the nations will accept the New World Order."

—David Rockefeller, in a statement to the United Nations Business Council, 1994.

"If we have to use force, it is because we are America. We are the indispensable nation."

—Secretary of State Madeleine Albright, 1995.

"Because of the value that comes from the ambiguity of what the U.S. may do to an adversary if the acts we seek to deter are carried out, it hurts to portray ourselves as too fully rational and cool-headed. The fact that some elements may appear to be potentially 'out of control' can be beneficial to creating and reinforcing fears and doubts within the minds of an adversary's decision makers. This essential sense of fear is the working force of deterrence. That the U.S. may become irrational and vindictive if its vital interests are attacked should be a part of the national persona we project to all adversaries."

—Excerpt from *Essentials of Post-Cold War Deterrence,* a study by the U.S. Strategic Command, March 1998.

"If [the Iraqis] turn on their radars we're going to blow up their goddamn SAMs. They know we own their country. We own their airspace. . . . We dictate the way they live and talk. And that's what's great about America right now. It's a good thing, especially when there's a lot of oil out there we need."

—U.S. Brigadier General William Looney, 1999.

"I'm going to kick Saddam Hussein's sorry motherfucking ass all over the Mideast."

—George W. Bush, speaking to members of his campaign staff, 1999.

"The hidden hand of the market will never work without a hidden fist—McDonald's cannot flourish without McDonnell Douglas, the designer of the F-15."

—Thomas L. Friedman, "A Manifesto for the Fast World," March 1999.

"NO! I don't care what the international lawyers say—we are going to kick some ass!"

—President George W. Bush, on the evening of September 11, 2001, when he was advised that international law does not allow the use of force for purposes of retaliation.

"At some point we might be the only ones left. That's okay with me. We're America."

—President George W. Bush, when told by Colin Powell that U.S. allies were not backing Bush's plans to invade Iraq, October 2001.

"Because Afghanistan was not enough. The radical Islamists want to humiliate us, and we need to humiliate them."

—Henry Kissinger, when asked why he supported the invasion of Iraq, April 2003.

"Every ten years or so, the United States needs to pick up some small crappy little country and throw it against the wall, just to show the world we mean business."

—Michael Ledeen, Freedom Scholar at the American Enterprise Institute, January 1992, as paraphrased by Jonah Goldberg in *National Review Online*, April 23, 2002.

"Not just equal time. It is dominion we are after, world conquest. That's what Christ has commissioned us to accomplish, and we must never settle for anything less."

—Reverend D. James Kennedy, pastor of Coral Ridge Presbyterian Church in Fort Lauderdale, Florida, 2005.

Space Dominance

"Whoever has the capability to control space will likewise possess the capability to exert control of the surface of the earth."

—General Thomas D. White, Air Force chief of staff, November 29, 1957.

"Some people don't want to hear this, and it sure isn't in vogue, but—absolutely—we're going to fight in space. We're going to fight from space and we're going to fight into space. . . . We will engage terrestrial targets someday—ships, airplanes, land targets—from space."

—Joseph W. Ashy, commander in chief of U.S. Space Command, August 1996.

"In the next two decades, new technologies will allow the fielding of space-based weapons of devastating effectiveness to be used to deliver energy and mass as force projection in tactical and strategic conflict. . . . These advances will enable lasers with reasonable mass and cost to effect very many kills."

—U.S. Air Force, *New World Vistas: Air and Space Power for the 21st Century*, 1996.

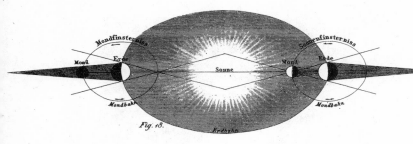

Fig. 18.

"With regard to space dominance, we have it, we like it, and we're going to keep it."

—Keith Hall, assistant secretary of the Air Force for Space, 1997.

"Historically, military forces have evolved to protect national interests and investments—both military and economic. . . . During the early portion of the 21st century, space power will also evolve into a separate and equal medium of warfare."

—U.S. Space Command, "Vision for 2020," 1998. U.S. Space Command was created by the Pentagon to coordinate the efforts of the Army, Navy, and Air Force to "institutionalize the use of space."

"Only the United States can be trusted to regulate space for the benefit of all."

—Professor Everett Dolman of the School of Advanced Air & Space Studies, the U.S. Air Force's graduate school for airpower at Maxwell Air Force Base, Alabama, 1998.

"Space offers attractive options not only for missile defense but for a broad range of interrelated civil and military missions. It truly is the ultimate high ground. We are exploring concepts and techniques for space-based intercepts."

—Paul Wolfowitz, Deputy Secretary of Defense, October 2002.

"Space superiority is our day-to-day mission. Space supremacy is our vision for the future. Simply put, it's the American way of fighting. . . . We must have freedom to attack as well as freedom from attack. Space superiority is not our birthright, but it is our destiny."

—General Lance Lord, head of Air Force Space Command, September 2004.

"Our vision calls for prompt global space strike systems with the capacity to directly apply force from or through space against terrestrial targets."

—U.S. Air Force Space Command, *Strategic Master Plan, Federal Year 2004 & Beyond.*

War and Peace

"In strict confidence, I should welcome almost any war, for I think this country needs one."

"The burning of New York and a few other sea coast cities would be a good object lesson in the need of an adequate system of coast defenses."

"The clamor of the peace faction in the United States has convinced me that this country needs a war. Peace comes not to the coward or to the timid, but to him who will do no wrong and is too strong to allow others to wrong him."

"I believe in 'just' wars. America is a 'just' nation. Therefore, any war she fights is 'just.'"

"America will never start a war if she can have what she wants without it. But if she cannot get what she wants and do as she pleases without war, then she must and will fight, for it would be dishonorable to let any nation or group of nations tell America what she can or cannot do."

"All the great masterful races have been fighting races. No triumph of peace is quite so great as the supreme triumphs of war. Diplomacy is utterly useless when there is no force behind it. It is through strife, or the readiness through strife, that a nation must win greatness."

—Theodore Roosevelt, 1897–1902.

"If we see that Germany is winning we ought to help Russia, and if Russia is winning we ought to help Germany, and that way let them kill as many as possible."

—Senator Harry S. Truman, 1941.

"I shall make of them the greatest slaughter in the history of mankind."

—General Douglas MacArthur, speaking about the Chinese entering the Korean War, October 1950.

"War with Russia is inevitable. We must blow them off the face of the earth quick, before they do the same to us—we haven't much time."

—Senator Brian McMahon, chairman of the Special Committee on Atomic Energy, 1951.

"Korea has been a blessing. There had to be a Korea either here or someplace in the world."

—General James Van Fleet, January 1951.

"Korea came along and saved us."

—Secretary of State Dean Acheson, February 1952.

"I don't think we can get much out of a Korean settlement until we have shown—before all Asia—our clear superiority by giving the Chinese one hell of a licking."

—Secretary of State John Foster Dulles, January 1953.

"Stop the aggression or we're going to bomb you into the Stone Age."

—Air Force General Curtis E. LeMay, urging President Lyndon Johnson to issue an ultimatum to North Vietnam, November 1965.

"They say, 'Well, these trucks are moving targets; you've got to be able to see them to hit them.' Bullshit! Just, just, just cream the fuckers!"

—President Richard M. Nixon, February 1971, raging at the U.S. Air Force for not stopping traffic on the Ho Chi Minh Trail.

"Those bastards are going to be bombed like they've never been bombed before! . . . We're gonna level that goddam country! I wanna know how many Japanese died in the nuclear bombardments. How many in the atomic bombings of Nagasaki and Hiroshima."

—President Richard M. Nixon, November 1971.

"That's the best investment in foreign assistance that the United States has made in my political life."

—President Richard M. Nixon, December 1971, referring to the United States spending $340 million a year bombing Cambodia. According to CIA figures, 600,000 Cambodians were killed during the bombing, and millions more became homeless.

President Richard M. Nixon: "I still think we ought to take the dikes out now. Will that drown people?"

Secretary of State Henry Kissinger: "That would drown about 200,000 people."

Nixon: "Well, no, no, no. I'd rather use the nuclear bomb."

Kissinger: "That, I think, would just be too much."

Nixon: "The nuclear bomb? Does that bother you?"

Kissinger: [Inaudible].

Nixon: "I just want you to think big, Henry, for Christ's sake."

—Conversation recorded in the Oval Office of the White House, April 25, 1972.

"We owe them no debt because the destruction was mutual."

—President Jimmy Carter, March 1977. Carter had been asked by a reporter about U.S. responsibility for the extensive devastation carried out in Vietnam.

"Peace is anathema to any company heavily involved in defense. The end of the Vietnam War wasn't good news. The recent outbreaks of peace were just as bad."

—Article in the *Financial Times*, August 11, 1990.

Lesley Stahl: "We have heard that half a million [Iraqi] children have died. That is more than died in Hiroshima. And, you know, is the price worth it?"

Secretary of State Madeleine Albright: "I think this is a very hard choice. But the price—we think the price is worth it."

—An exchange on CBS's *60 Minutes*, May 1996.

"One of the keys to being seen as a great leader is to be seen as a commander in chief. My father had all this political capital built up when he drove the Iraqis out of Kuwait and he wasted it. If I ever get the chance to invade, I'm not going to waste it."

—George W. Bush to author Mickey Herskowitz in 1999, while campaigning for the Republican nomination for president.

"I'm going to take him out!"

—George W. Bush to Osama Siblani, editor of *The Arab American News*, referring to Saddam Hussein, while campaigning for the Republican nomination for president, 1999.

"When we're through with them, they'll have flies walking across their eyeballs."

—Cofer Black, director of the CIA's Counterterrorism Center, during a presentation to President Bush about the war against Al Qaeda in Afghanistan, September 13, 2001.

"We'll bomb you back to the Stone Age."

—Deputy Secretary of State Richard Armitage, explaining to Pakistani President Musharraf what would happen if Pakistan didn't cooperate with America's interests in the Middle East, September 2001.

"To Iran, Syria, Saudi Arabia, Lebanon, and the PLO, we could deliver a short message, a two-word message: 'You're next.'"

—Richard Perle, chairman of the George W. Bush administration's Defense Policy Advisory Board, April 2003.

"This is total war. If we just let our vision of the world go forth and we embrace it entirely and we don't try to piece together clever diplomacy but just wage a total war, our children will sing great songs about us years from now."

—Richard Perle, February 2005.

"Creative destruction is our middle name, both within our society and abroad. We must destroy our enemies to advance our historic mission. We must be imperious, ruthless, and relentless until there is total surrender in the Middle East. We must keep our fangs bared. We must remind them daily that we Americans are in a rage, and we will not rest until we have avenged our dead, we will not be sated until we have had the blood of every miserable little tyrant in the Middle East, and every last drooling, anti-Semitic and anti-American mullah, imam, sheikh, and ayatollah is either singing the praise of the United States of America or pumping gasoline, for a dime a gallon, on an American military base near the Arctic Circle."

"One can only hope that we turn the region into a cauldron, and faster, please."

—Michael Ledeen, neoconservative political analyst, December 2005.

"Money trumps peace."

—President George W. Bush, February 2007.

Communism
and the Cold War

"There are apostles of Lenin in our own midst. I cannot imagine what it means to be an apostle of Lenin. It means to be an apostle of the night, of chaos, of disorder."

—President Woodrow Wilson, April 1919.

"I thank heaven for a man like Adolph Hitler, who built a front line of defense against the Antichrist of communism."

—Christian missionary Francis X. Buchman, April 1936.

"The Russians are like people from across the tracks whose manners are very bad."

—President Harry S. Truman, August 1945.

"It was perfectly clear to us that if we told the Japanese to lay down their arms immediately and march to the seaboard, the entire country would be taken over by the communists. We therefore had to take the unusual step of using the enemy as a garrison until we could airlift Chinese National troops to South China and send U.S. Marines to guard the seaports."

—President Harry S. Truman, explaining why the United States allowed Japanese soldiers, still in China at the end of World War II, to fight against the Chinese communists, 1945.

"He's a communist."

—President Harry S. Truman, February 1946, explaining why he thought Pablo Picasso should never be allowed into the U.S.

"[W]here the concepts and traditions of popular government are too weak to absorb successfully the intensity of the communist attack, then we must concede that harsh governmental measures of repression may be the only answer; that these measures may have to proceed from regimes whose origins and methods would not stand the test of American concepts of democratic procedures; and that such regimes and such methods may be preferable alternatives, and indeed the only alternatives, to further communist success."

—George F. Kennan, head of the U.S. State Department's Policy Planning Staff, 1947.

"The communists will understand the lash when it's put to them."

—General Emmet "Rosie" O'Donnell, 1949.

"The Russians are the heirs of Mongol killers . . . the greatest killers in the history of the world."

—President Harry S. Truman, 1950.

"The poor people are the ones [the communists] appeal to and they've always wanted to plunder the rich."

"We are confronted by an unfortunate fact. Most of the countries of the world do not share our view that communist control of any government anywhere is in itself a danger and a threat."

—Secretary of State John Foster Dulles, 1954.

"Atomic weapons should be employed to create a belt of scorched earth across the avenues of communism to block the Asiatic hordes."

—Advice to the Eisenhower administration by General Charles Willoughby, General Douglas MacArthur's Director of Intelligence, 1954.

"We could drop three small tactical A-bombs . . . and clean those commies out of there and the band could play the 'Marseillaise' and the French would come marching out of Dien Bien Phu in fine shape."

—Air Force Chief of Staff Nathan Twining, speaking in support of Secretary of State John Foster Dulles's suggestion of U.S. bombing to save the French forces at Dien Bien Phu in Vietnam, 1954.

"Governments of the military type of El Salvador are the most effective in containing communism in Latin America."

—President John F. Kennedy, 1961.

"I cut his balls off."

—President John F. Kennedy, to friends in November 1962, referring to his confrontation with Nikita Khrushchev during the Cuban Missile Crisis of October 1962. In fact, however, JFK had made a secret deal with Khruschev, which allowed him to come out of the situation looking as if he had forced the Soviets to back down.

"We lost! We ought to just go in there today and knock 'em off!"

—Colonel Curtis E. LeMay, chief of staff of the U.S. Air Force in October 1962, after the United States and USSR had peacefully settled the Cuban Missile Crisis.

"I can't let Vietnam go to the communists and then go and ask these people [the U.S. public] to reelect me. Somehow we've got to hold that territory through the '64 elections. But we've got no future there. The South Vietnamese hate us, they want us out of there. At one point they'll kick our asses out of there."

—President John F. Kennedy, confiding to friends in August 1963.

"I didn't just screw Ho Chi Minh, I cut off his pecker."

—President Lyndon B. Johnson, to a member of the media, just after he had announced the start of Operation Rolling Thunder, the sustained bombing of North Vietnam, 1965.

"I call it the Madman Theory, Bob. I want the North Vietnamese to believe I've reached the point where I might do *anything* to stop the war. We'll just slip the word to them that, 'For God's sake, you know Nixon is obsessed about communists. We can't restrain him when he's angry—and he has his hand on the nuclear button'—and Ho Chi Minh himself will be in Paris in two days begging for peace."

—President Richard M. Nixon, to White House chief of staff H.R. "Bob" Haldeman, 1969.

"The question in the beginning was, 'Is it right for the United States to give weapons to people who wind up being killed in order to keep the Russians off balance?' I thought that was a tough question, morally, to answer. The whole program of feeding freedom fighters is one of feeding people who cannot win militarily. But at the time, back in 1979, there was surely a benefit to the United States in this. So I said, 'Okay. I think I can morally accept this.'"

—CIA Director Stansfield Turner, defending his decision to have the CIA secretly supply weapons and supplies to the *mujaheddin* fighting the Russians in Afghanistan, 1979.

"Eat shit, commie faggot."

"I want to fuck communism out of this little island, and fuck it right back to Moscow."

—Written on the walls of the residence of the Cuban ambassador to Grenada by U.S. Marines during the invasion of Grenada in 1983.

"There were 58,000 dead in Vietnam and we owe the Russians one. . . . I have a slight obsession with it, because of Vietnam. I thought the Soviets ought to get a dose of it. . . . The Russians have lost maybe 25,000 in Afghanistan. I figure they owe us 33,000 dead."

—Representative Charles Wilson of Texas in 1985, justifying the U.S. government's massive support of the Afghan rebels in their struggle against the Soviet Union from 1979 to 1988.

"It's too bad it didn't happen closer to the Kremlin."

—Senator Steve Symms of Idaho, reacting to the news of the Chernobyl disaster, 1986.

"No one cared, as long as they were communists, that they were being butchered. No one was getting very worked up about it. . . . They probably killed a lot of people, and I probably have a lot of blood on my hands, but that's not all bad."

—Howard Federspiel, 1990. In 1965 Federspiel was a U.S. State Department expert on intelligence in Indonesia and had helped the CIA supply lists to the Indonesian military of thousands of people to be killed. It's estimated that over 500,000 Indonesians were slaughtered during this period.

"I enjoyed killing communists. I liked to kill communists any way I could get them. . . . They said Indonesia was a failure. But we knocked the shit out of them. We killed thousands of communists, even though half of them probably didn't know what communism meant."

—Al Pope, in a 2005 interview, speaking about his role as a CIA pilot in the secret bombing of Indonesia in 1958. Pope was personally responsible for the bombing of a church and a marketplace, killing many civilians.

Weapons of
Mass Destruction

"God Almighty in His infinite wisdom [has] dropped the atomic bomb in our lap. It's our opportunity right now to compel mankind to adopt the policy of lasting peace or be burned to a crisp."

—Colorado Senator Edwin Johnson, 1945.

"I think that the plutonium from the thousands of bombs scattered universally over the earth would do us all good (stimulates the spermocytes—not for publication). Plutonium, next to alcohol, is probably one of the better things in life."

—Louis Hempleman, Atomic Energy Commission scientist, 1946.

"The radioactive casualty can be of several causes. He can have a smaller amount which will cause him to die rather soon, and as I understand it from the doctors, without undue suffering. In fact, they say it is a very pleasant way to die."

—Brigadier General Leslie R. Groves, head of the Manhattan Project, testifying before the Senate Select Committee on Atomic Energy, 1946.

"I think our position in this matter of human experimentation is the same as everybody else. We don't want to do it if we can get out of doing it, but if that is the only way we can get the answer, that certainly is going to be more economical in the long run, to take a few chances now and perhaps not lose a battle, or even worse than that, lose a war."

—U.S. Navy Admiral Frederick Greaves, 1950.

"It would be feasible to risk an all-out atomic attack at the beginning of a war in an effort to stun the enemy into submission."

—General Curtis E. LeMay, head of Strategic Air Command, 1948.

"Fear of radiation is almost universal among the uninitiated, and unless it is overcome in the military forces, it could present a most serious problem if atomic weapons are used for tactical or strategic purposes. . . . A tactical exercise of this nature would clearly demonstrate that persistent ionizing radiation following an atomic explosion presents no hazards to personnel and equipment and would effectively dispel a fear that is dangerous and demoralizing but entirely groundless. The necessity of destroying this fear is considered to be of great importance and should be accorded the highest priority possible."

—Richard Meiling, chairman of the Armed Forces Medical Policy Council, a powerful group within the Office of the Secretary of Defense, in a June 1951 memo urging that soldiers be marched into Ground Zero immediately following nuclear bomb tests at the Atomic Testing Site at Camp Desert Rock, Nevada. During these tests, which took place from 1951 to 1961, approximately 300,000 enlisted men were ordered to take part.

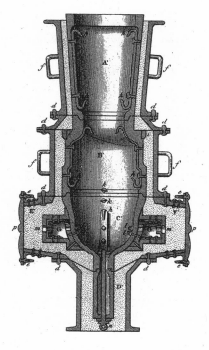

"Radiation will not hurt you; even if it passes over your trench by a fraction of an inch, you'll be safe."

—Part of the training instructions given to GIs participating in nuclear bomb tests at the Atomic Testing Site in Nevada, 1951.

"It was a memorable experience for the men, and much of the superstition and mystery surrounding radiation was removed. They are [now] convinced that the [blast] area can be safely entered after the explosion; that effects decrease rapidly with distance; and, most important, of the life-saving protection of a hole in the ground at any distance from ground zero."

—From a 1951 report by the Human Resources Research Office of George Washington University, which was given a military contract to perform psychological studies of the GIs' attitudes and reactions during nuclear bomb tests.

"I see a unique use for the atomic bomb—to strike a blocking blow—which would require a six-month repair job. Sweeten up my B-29 force."

—General Douglas MacArthur, commander of United Nations forces in Korea, 1951.

"Unless China pulls back its forces, we should give them a taste of the atom."

—U.S. Secretary of Defense George Marshall, explaining how he was going to advise President Eisenhower after visiting Korea in June 1951.

"The peoples of Korea and China have indeed been the objectives of bacteriological weapons. These have been employed by units of the U.S.A. armed forces, using a great variety of different methods for the purpose, some of which seem to be developments of those applied by the Japanese during the Second World War.... Among the array of germ weapons used were feathers infected with anthrax; lice, fleas, and mosquitoes dosed with plague and yellow fever; diseased rodents; and various implements contaminated with deadly microbes—toilet paper, envelopes, and the ink in fountain pens."

—Excerpt of a 1952 report by a United Nations "International Scientific Committee," formed to investigate claims by the Chinese government that the United States had used germ warfare in northern Korea and northeast China.

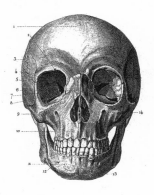

"Under conditions of a tower explosion, such as currently being conducted in the Nevada tests, it may be possible to place troops in deep foxholes as close as 800 feet from Ground Zero without these troops suffering serious injury."

—Colonel John Oakes, secretary of the Army General Staff, 1953.

"It's not dangerous."

—Walter Cronkite, commenting to his television audience about the radioactive cloud drifting off-camera during a nationally televised 1953 atomic test in Nevada.

"Because of the prevailing winds, it would take the [fallout] up to about the 80,000-foot level, way up in the stratosphere. Sometimes the fallout would go twice around the earth. . . . Any bomb that was set off in the United States, the odds were pretty great that a large portion of the fallout would be in Russia. In fact, there was a project that was highly classified to see if we couldn't increase the fallout over Russia."

—Dr. John Willard, who worked with the Manhattan Project and later at the Nevada Atomic Test Site, 1953.

"I'm personally convinced that smoking is either helping or is the main cause. If uranium miners never smoked, we would never have known there was a problem."

—Dr. Robert W. Buechley, 1954, in charge of a study group authorized by Union Carbide Company to investigate claims by mine workers that conditions in uranium mines were causing lung cancer.

"Yes, the work was dangerous, but no real harm had been done."

—Lewis Strauss, chairman of the Atomic Energy Commission, testifying to a 1954 congressional committee investigating reports showing that severely high death rates from cancer and heart disease among uranium mine workers were caused by radiation exposure.

"Because the issue was complicated and there was no certified proof that radiation in the mines killed miners, no action should be taken."

—Final report issued in 1954 by the previously cited congressional committee.

"People have got to learn to live with the facts of life, and part of the facts of life are fallout."

—W. F. Libby, commissioner of the Atomic Energy Commission, 1955.

"There isn't anybody in the United States who isn't a 'downwinder.' . . . When we followed the clouds, we went all over the United States from east to west and covering a broad spectrum of Mexico and Canada."

—U.S. Air Force Colonel Langdon Harrison, 1956. Harrison spent years sampling the fallout from nuclear tests. His reports remain classified to this day.

"Distant or worldwide radioactive fallout is not a controlling factor in bomb testing. To permit us to fall behind the Russians is disastrous; to wait for them to catch up to us is stupid."

—Shields Warren, director of the Atomic Energy Commission's Division of Biology and Medicine, in a 1956 telegram to AEC Director Lewis Strauss.

"The sun, not the bomb, is your worst enemy at Camp Desert Rock."

—*Camp Desert Rock Information Book*, the instruction guide given to all GIs participating in nuclear bomb tests in Nevada, 1957.

"If anybody knows how to do a good job of body snatching, they will really be serving their country."

—Willard Libby, head of the Atomic Energy Commission's "Operation Sunshine," a program to gather samples of human bones, entire skeletons and human fetuses from around the world to determine just how much radiation had been spread due to atomic testing, 1958.

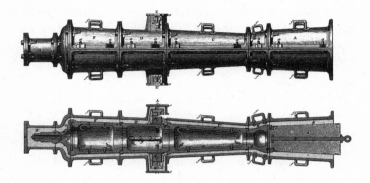

"Just what the hell do you think you're doing, saying the amount of radiation we're allowing is causing cancer? I've been assured by the Atomic Energy Commission people that a dose of a hundred times what they're allowing won't hurt anybody. Listen, there have been lots of guys before you who tried to interfere with the AEC program. We got them and we'll get you."

—Representative Chet Holifield of California, chairman of the U.S. Congress's Joint Committee on Atomic Energy, to Drs. John Gofman and Arthur Tamplin, who testified to the committee of the terrible dangers of atomic radiation, January 1970.

"The experiments were invaluable. We learned so much from them. I'm truly sorry you lost your husband. . . . I just wanted you to know all of us have benefited from those tests. They were worthwhile, and the men who died were not sacrificed in vain."

—A U.S. Army colonel, after a congressional hearing in 1970. The wife of a GI who had died as the result of radiation exposure during atomic bomb tests in Nevada had asked him, "What good was served when 300,000 men were ordered to participate in atomic weapons testing where many have died and others are dying currently as a result of their exposure to radiation?"

"[We were] always on the lookout for somebody who had some kind of terminal disease who was going to undergo an amputation. These things were not done to plague people or make them sick and miserable. They were not done to kill people. They were done to gain potentially valuable information. The fact that they were injected [with plutonium] and provided this valuable data could almost be a sort of memorial rather than something to be ashamed of. It doesn't bother me to talk about the plutonium injectees because of the value of the information they provided."

—Scientist Patricia Durbin of California, commenting in 1971 on the Atomic Energy Commission's experiments with plutonium injections into unknowing test subjects during the 1950s and 1960s.

"You have a [nuclear] capability that inflicts more damage on the opposition than it can inflict upon you. That's the way you can have a winner."

—Vice President George H. W. Bush, 1983.

"Plutonium's dangerous, but there's also enough water in Lake Tahoe to drown everybody in the state of California if you could put it into their lungs. Well, plutonium has the same problem. You mustn't get it in everybody's lungs."

—Spokesman for General Electric, 1991.

"Free nations are peaceful nations. Free nations don't attack each other. Free nations don't develop weapons of mass destruction."

—President George W. Bush, October 2003.

Ethnic Equality

"The gradual extension of our settlements will as certainly cause the savage, as the wolf, to retire; both being beasts of prey, tho' they differ in shape."

"These Indians are merely animals of prey."

—George Washington, after unleashing attacks on Native Americans during the Revolutionary War.

"As slaves multiply so fast . . . it is cheaper to raise than import them. . . . [But] let us not intermeddle. As population increases, poor laborers will be so plenty as to render slaves useless."

—Oliver Ellsworth of Connecticut, one of the "Founding Fathers," 1787.

"It will perhaps cause [the Indians], gradually, under the protection of the government and through the influence of good counsels, to cast off their savage habits and become an interesting, civilized, and Christian community."

—President Andrew Jackson, in his second annual Message to Congress in December 1830, speaking of the Indian Removal Act, the U.S. government's forced removal of the Cherokee Indians from their Georgia homelands to make room for white settlers.

"The Mexicans are a pusillanimous race of men, and unfit to control the destinies of that beautiful country."

—Attorney T. J. Farnham, in his popular 1840 book, *Travels in the Great Western Prairies.*

"The Indians of California make as obedient and humble slaves as the Negro in the South."

—Pierson Reading, a manager of John Sutter's huge grant of Indian land in central California, 1844.

"The Mexicans are an idle, thriftless people."

—Author Richard Dana, 1845.

"[The Mexicans are] a wretched people; wretched in their origin, history, and character, who must eventually give way as the Indians did. . . . The United States should expand not by war, rather by the power of her ideas . . . by the steady advance of a superior race, with superior ideas and a better civilization . . . by being better than Mexico, wiser, humaner, more free and manly."

—Reverend Theodore Parker, Unitarian minister in Boston, 1846.

"Are we prepared to place on a perfect equality with us, in social and political position, the half-breeds and mongrels of Mexico? The idea is revolting."

—Editorial in the *Richmond Times*, 1846.

"I am afraid of Americans mingling with an inferior people, who embrace all shades of color . . . a sad compound of Spanish, English, Indian, and Negro bloods . . . and resulting, it is said, in the production of a slothful, ignorant race of beings."

—Congressman Stephen Delano of Ohio, explaining why he was opposed to war with Mexico, 1846.

"The African race in the United States, even when free, are everywhere a degraded class, and exercise no political influence. The privileges they are allowed to enjoy are accorded to them as a matter of kindness and benevolence rather than of right. . . . They were not looked upon as citizens by the contracting parties who formed the Constitution. They were evidently not supposed to be included by the term 'citizens.'"

—U.S. Supreme Court Chief Justice Roger Taney of Maryland, defending his decision in the Dred Scott Case, 1856.

"I will say, then, that I am not, nor ever have been, in favor of bringing about in any way the social and political equality of the white and black races; that I am not, nor ever have been, in favor of making voters or jurors of Negroes, nor of qualifying them to hold office, nor to intermarry with white people. . . . And inasmuch as they cannot so live, while they do remain together there must be the position of superior and inferior, and I as much as any other man am in favor of having the superior position assigned to the white race."

—Abraham Lincoln, in a speech given in southern Illinois during his 1858 campaign for the Senate.

"In my opinion, this government of ours is founded on the white basis. It was made by white men, for the benefit of white men, to be administered by white men. . . . I am opposed to taking any step that recognizes the Negro man or the Indian as the equal of the white man."

—Senator Stephen A. Douglas, July 1858.

"I have no purpose, directly or indirectly, to interfere with the institution of slavery in the States where it exists. I believe I have no lawful right to do so, and I have no inclination to do so."

—President Abraham Lincoln, in his first Inaugural Address, March 1861.

"When dealing with savage men, as with savage beasts, no question of national honor can arise. Whatever action the U.S. government cares to take is solely a part of expediency."

—Francis A. Walker, commissioner of Indian Affairs, 1871.

"The best way to control the nigger is to whip him when he does not obey without it."

—James K. Vardaman, governor of Mississippi, 1888.

"There is no use to equivocate or lie about the matter. Mississippi's constitutional convention of 1890 was held for no other reason than to eliminate the nigger from politics. Let the world know it just as it is."

—James K. Vardaman, governor of Mississippi, 1890.

"With Sitting Bull's fall, the nobility of the redskin is exterminated, and what few are left are a pack of whining curs who lick the hand that smites them. The whites, by law of conquest, by justice of civilization, are masters of the American continent, and the best safety of the frontier will be secured by the total annihilation of the few remaining Indians. Why annihilation? Their glory has fled, their spirit broken, their manhood effaced; better they die than live as the miserable wretches they are."

—L. Frank Baum, in the December 20, 1890 edition of the *Aberdeen Saturday Pioneer*. (Baum later wrote the famous *Oz* children's stories.)

"The Indian child is of lower physical organization than the white child of corresponding age. His forearms are smaller and his fingers and hands are less flexible. The very structure of his bones and muscles will not permit so wide a variety of manual movements as are customary among Caucasian children, and his very instincts and modes of thought are adjusted to his imperfect manual development."

—Estelle Reed, U.S. superintendent of Indian Schools, appointed by President William McKinley, 1898.

"The action of President Roosevelt in entertaining that nigger will necessitate our killing a thousand niggers in the South before they will learn their place again."

—Senator Benjamin "Pitchfork" Tillman of South Carolina, commenting on President Theodore Roosevelt's inviting Booker T. Washington to have dinner in the White House, 1901.

"I'm in my glory when I can sight my gun on some dark skin and pull the trigger."

—U.S. marine in the Philippine Islands, 1901.

"Our fighting blood was up, and we all wanted to kill 'niggers.' . . . This shooting human beings beats rabbit hunting all to pieces."

—Volunteer soldier from the state of Washington writing home about his experiences in the U.S. war against Filipino insurrectionists, 1901.

"We exterminated the American Indians, and I guess most of us are proud of it, or, at least, believe the end justifies the means; and we must have no scruples about exterminating this other race standing in the way of progress and enlightenment, if it is necessary."

—U.S. soldier active in the Philippines, 1901.

"It may be necessary to kill half the Filipinos in order that the remaining half of the population may be advanced to a higher plane of life."

—General Benjamin Shafter, U.S. field commander in the Philippine Islands, 1901.

"Senators must remember that we are not dealing with Americans or Europeans, we are dealing with Orientals."

—Senator Albert J. Beveridge of Massachusetts, when the Senate was apprised of atrocities carried out by U.S. troops in the Philippines during the Spanish-American War, 1901.

"[The United States should take the Philippines] in the interests of the white race. . . . To grant self-government to the Philippines under Aguinaldo would be like granting self-government to an Apache reservation under some local chief."

—Vice President Theodore Roosevelt, 1901.

"Democracy has justified itself by keeping for the white race the best portions of the new world's surface. . . . The superior white race must bear the burden of civilizing colonial peoples of the world, if necessary, against the will of those people."

"The Chinese must be kept out of America because their presence here would be ruinous to the white race."

"Now, as to the Negroes! I entirely agree with you that as a race and in the mass [they] are altogether inferior to the whites."

—President Theodore Roosevelt, 1902–1904.

"They [the Haitians] are an inferior people, unable to maintain the degree of civilization left them by the French or to develop any capacity of self-government entitling them to international respect and confidence."

—Assistant Secretary of State William Phillips, 1912.

"Dear me, think of it, niggers speaking French."

—Secretary of State William Jennings Bryan, commenting about the elite of Haitian society, 1914.

"The experience of Liberia and Haiti show that the African race is devoid of any capacity for political organization and lack genius for government. Unquestionably there is an inherent tendency to revert to savagery and to cast aside the shackles of civilization which are irksome to their physical nature. Of course, there are many exceptions to this racial weakness, but it is true of the mass, as we know from experience in this country. It is that which makes the Negro problem practically unsolvable."

—Secretary of State Robert Lansing, 1915.

"It is like writing history with lightning, and my only regret is that it is all so true."

—President Woodrow Wilson, 1915, after viewing a private White House showing of D.W. Griffith's film, *Birth of a Nation*, one of the most racist movies of all time, and condemned by the NAACP as racially inflammatory.

"I know the nigger and how to handle him. . . . [The Haitian people] are real niggers and no mistake—there are some very fine looking, well-educated, polished men here, but they are real nigs beneath the surface."

—U.S. Marine Colonel Littleton W. T. Waller, in a 1916 memo to a superior officer, after leading the first U.S. forces to occupy Haiti in 1916.

"I believe that the white man of western Europe is the most able and progressive of earth's types, and that the men of the United States are the most able group of the western European stock. I believe that the yellow and red men are less able, and the black men least of all."

—Captain John Houston Craige of the U.S. Marines, who served as the U.S. occupation forces' chief of police in Port-au-Prince, Haiti in 1916.

"It is well to distinguish at once between the Dominicans and the Haitians. The former, while in many ways not advanced far enough for the highest type of self-government, yet have a preponderance of white blood and culture. The Haitians on the other hand are Negro for the most part, and, barring a very few highly educated politicians, are almost in a state of savagery and complete ignorance."

—Secretary of State Robert Lansing, 1917.

"Any man who carries a hyphen about with him carries a dagger that he is ready to plunge into the vitals of this republic whenever he gets ready."

—President Woodrow Wilson, 1918. Wilson referred to anyone who was not a native-born American as a "Hyphenated American."

"The Puerto Ricans are the dirtiest, laziest, most degenerate and thievish race of men ever inhabiting this sphere. . . . I have done my best to further the process of extermination by killing off eight and transplanting cancer into several more. . . . All physicians take delight in the abuse and torture of the unfortunate subjects."

—Cornelius Rhoads, chief pathologist of the Rockefeller Institute, who in 1931 oversaw an experiment that deliberately infected Puerto Rican subjects with cancer, causing 13 deaths. Dr. Rhoads was never prosecuted for his crimes, but was declared to be "mentally ill." The U.S. government, however, must have disagreed with this diagnosis, as it placed Rhoads in charge of two large chemical warfare projects during the 1940s, granting him a seat on the Atomic Energy Commission, and later awarding him with a Legion of Merit medal.

"If it were a question of having a Marine Corps of 5,000 whites or 250,000 Negroes, I would rather have the whites."

—Major General Thomas Holcomb, Marine Corps commandant, 1941.

"The best way to keep a nigger away from a white primary is to see him the night before."

—Theodore G. Bilbo, governor of North Carolina, 1945.

"The Jews claim God Almighty picked them out for special privilege. Well, I'm sure he had better judgment."

"Jesus Christ couldn't please them [the Jews] when he was here on Earth, so how could anyone expect that I would have better luck?"

—President Harry S. Truman, July 1946.

"The best way to handle Latin Americans is by patting them a little bit and make them think that you are fond of them."

—Secretary of State John Foster Dulles, June 1952.

"We thought we could knock off these little brown people on the cheap."

—A CIA official, commenting on the $20 million it cost to run its Operation PBSUCCESS, the violent overthrow of the democratically elected government of Guatemala, in 1954.

"These four mongrels were supposed to be our defense against communism and the extremes of Arab nationalism in the Middle East."

—Harrison Symmes, U.S. ambassador to Jordan, September 1957. Symmes was referring to U.S. dealings with King Saud of Saudi Arabia, King Hussein of Jordan, President Camille Chamoun of Lebanon, and President Nuri Said of Iraq.

"If Chief Justice Earl Warren and his associates had known God's word, the [1954 Supreme Court ruling which desegregated public schools] *Brown v. Board of Education* decision would never have been made. The facilities should be separate. When God has drawn a line of distinction, we should not attempt to cross that line. The true Negro does not want integration. His potential is far better among his own race."

—Reverend Jerry Falwell, speaking to his congregation at the Thomas Road Baptist Church, 1958.

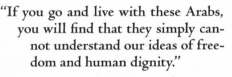

"If you go and live with these Arabs, you will find that they simply cannot understand our ideas of freedom and human dignity."

—President Dwight D. Eisenhower, at a National Security Council meeting, June 1959.

"The goddamn Chinks."

—Walt Rostow, head of policy planning at the U.S. State Department during the Kennedy administration, 1961.

"They had to dig deep in the garbage for this one."

—FBI Director J. Edgar Hoover, after *Time* magazine named Martin Luther King, Jr. its "Man of the Year" for 1963.

"I am amazed that the Pope gave an audience to such a degenerate."

—FBI Director J. Edgar Hoover, 1964, speaking of Martin Luther King, Jr.

"Segregation now, segregation tomorrow, segregation forever."

—George Wallace, governor of Alabama, in his 1963 inaugural speech.

"We have to use overwhelming force because we are out-numbered 15-to-1 by people who are ready to sweep over the United States and take what we have. If we don't use our power we'll be easy prey to any yellow dwarf with a pocketknife."

—President Lyndon B. Johnson, 1964.

"I know my Latinos. They understand only two things—a buck in the pocket and a kick in the ass."

—Thomas C. Mann, advisor to President Lyndon Johnson at the time of the U.S. invasion of the Dominican Republic, 1965.

"[Agents] should bear in mind that the two things foremost in the militant Negro's mind are sex and money."

—1967 FBI memo to its agents in charge of secret operations against civil rights groups on how to be more effective against them.

"Edgar says no. He's not going to send the FBI in every time some nigger woman says she's been raped."

—Attorney General Tom Clark, after conferring with FBI Director J. Edgar Hoover regarding Bureau investigations of rapes of civil rights workers, 1968.

"You come here speaking of Latin America, but this is not important. Nothing important can come from the south. History has never been produced in the south. The axis of history starts in Moscow, goes to Bonn, crosses over to Washington, and then goes to Tokyo. What happens in the south is of no importance. You're wasting your time."

—National Security Advisor Henry Kissinger to Gabriel Valdés, foreign minister from Chile, after Valdés had talked with Kissinger and President Richard M. Nixon in the Oval Office in June 1969.

"These people are just down out of the trees."

—President Richard M. Nixon, referring to African diplomats visiting the White House, April 1970.

"I wonder what the dining room is going to smell like."

—National Security Advisor Henry Kissinger, regarding a White House dinner for African diplomats, April 1970.

"Let's leave the niggers to [Secretary of State] Bill [Rogers] and we'll take care of the rest of the world."

—President Richard M. Nixon to National Security Advisor Henry Kissinger, June 1970.

"Henry's my Jew-boy."

—President Richard M. Nixon, speaking of Henry Kissinger at a National Security Council meeting, October 1970.

"I didn't say I wouldn't go into ghetto areas. I've been in many of them, and to some extent I would say this: if you've seen one city slum, you've seen them all."

—Vice President Spiro Agnew, 1970.

"All the Jews seem to be the ones that are for liberalizing the regulations on marijuana."

—President Richard M. Nixon, March 1971.

Reverend Billy Graham: "This Jewish stranglehold has got to be broken or the country's going to go down the drain."

President Richard M. Nixon: "You believe that?"

Graham: "Yes, sir."

Nixon: "Oh, boy, so do I. I can't ever say it, but I believe it."

Graham: "No, but if you get elected a second time, then we might be able to do something. By the way, [*Time* Magazine editor-in-chief] Hedley Donovan has invited me to have lunch with [the *Time*] editors."

[White House Chief of Staff] H. R. Haldeman: "You better take your Jewish beanie."

Graham: "Is that right? I don't know any of them now. A lot of Jews are great friends of mine. They swarm around me and are friendly with me because they know that I'm friendly with Israel. But they don't know how I really feel about what they are doing to this country."

Nixon: "You must not let them know."

—Oval Office conversation, 1972.

"The only way to deal with the Indian problem in South Dakota is to put a gun to the leaders' heads and pull the trigger."

—South Dakota Attorney General William Janklow, during the U.S. government and American Indian Movement clashes at Pine Ridge, South Dakota, 1975.

"I know a few of you here today don't like Jews, and I know why. The Jew can make more money accidentally than you can on purpose."

—Reverend Jerry Falwell, speaking to his parishioners, 1979.

"That's the way it has always been; it's in the culture."

—Deane Hinton, U.S. ambassador to El Salvador, commenting to U.S. church organizations concerned with the level of government violence toward the citizenry in El Salvador, 1981.

"I'm not against the blacks, and a lot of the good blacks will attest to that."

—Evan Mecham, governor of Arizona, 1987.

"Blacks didn't come out for me like the Hispanics did. So they're not gonna see much help from me."

—George W. Bush, just after being elected
governor of Texas in 1994.

"If I see someone come in that's got a diaper on his head and a fan belt wrapped around the diaper on his head, that guy needs to be pulled over."

—John Cooksey, representative from Louisiana, February, 2002.

"Arrest every Muslim that crosses a state line."

—Saxby Chambliss, senator from Georgia, suggesting an antiterrorism
strategy, April 2003.

"I don't understand how they can call me anti-Latino when I've made four movies in Mexico."

—Arnold Schwarzenegger, governor of California, March 2004.

"Actually, it's quite fun to fight Muslims. It's a hell of a hoot. It's fun to shoot some people. Guys like that ain't got no manhood anyway. So it's a hell of a lot of fun to shoot them."

—Marine Lieutenant General James Mattis, to a group of military families gathered in San Diego, February 2005.

"You could abort every black baby in this country and your crime rate would go down."

—Bill Bennett, talk show host and former secretary of education in the Reagan administration, September 28, 2005.

"Why do they [Arabs] hate each other? Why do Sunnis kill Shiites? How do they tell the difference? They all look the same to me."

—Senator Trent Lott of Mississippi, September 28, 2006.

"Do I care if the Sunnis and Shiites kill each other in Iraq? No. I don't care. Let's get our people out of there. Let them kill each other. Maybe they'll all kill each other, and then we can have a decent country in Iraq."

—Bill O'Reilly, political commentator, December 5, 2006.

"America's not ready for an Affirmative Action presidency."

—Conservative talk show host Michael Savage, February 4, 2008.

"Al Sharpton was invited to the White House? I hope they nailed down all the valuables."

—Laura Ingraham, Fox News, February 13, 2008.

Gender Equality

"American women would be too wise to wrinkle their foreheads with politics."

—Thomas Jefferson, 1793.

"Sensible and responsible women do not want to vote."

—President Grover Cleveland, 1889.

"I cook occasionally, just to see how easy women's work is."

—Tip O'Neill, Speaker of the House, 1963.

"Women are hard enough to handle now without giving them a gun."

—Barry Goldwater, on women in the armed forces, while campaigning for president, September 1964.

"I'm not for women in any job. I don't want them around."

—President Richard M. Nixon, 1971.

"Women are no more than a pastime, a hobby."

—Secretary of State Henry Kissinger, 1972.

"I want to turn women loose on the environmental crisis. Nobody knows more about pollution when detergents back up in the kitchen sink."

—Vice President-elect Nelson Rockefeller, 1976.

"There are so many women on the floor of Congress, it looks like a mall."

—Illinois Representative Henry Hyde, 1977.

"Women are best suited for secretarial work, decorating cakes, and counter sales, like selling lingerie."

—South Carolina State Representative
Robert Dutton, June 1979.

"Damn it, when you get married, you kind of expect you're going to get a little sex."

—Alabama Senator Jeremiah Denton, 1986. Denton had offered a bill in the U.S. Senate to provide criminal immunity for the rape of a spouse.

"As long as it's inevitable, you might as well lie back and enjoy it."

—Clayton Williams, a Texas oilman who ran for governor of Texas in 1990. Williams was joking with reporters, equating a sudden thunderstorm to the recent rape of a Texas woman.

"Female militants are more of an object of ridicule and a pain in the butt than the black chauvinists."

—Pat Buchanan, Republican presidential candidate, 1996.

"The feminist agenda . . . is not about equal rights for women. It is about a socialist, anti-family, political movement that encourages women to leave their husbands, kill their children, practice witchcraft, and become lesbians."

—Reverend Pat Robertson, Republican candidate for president, 1998.

"If you talk about being in combat, what does combat mean? If combat means being in a ditch, females have biological problems being in a ditch for 30 days because they get infections, and they don't have upper body strength. I mean, some do, but they're relatively rare. On the other hand, men are basically little piglets. You drop them in a ditch, they roll around in it, doesn't matter, you know? These things are very real. On the other hand, if combat means being in an Aegis class cruiser managing the controls for 12 ships and their rockets, a female again may be dramatically better than a male, who gets very, very frustrated sitting in a chair all the time because males are biologically driven to go out and hunt giraffes."

—Speaker of the House Newt Gingrich, 1998.

"Pussy."

—George W. Bush, April 1999, when *Hartford Courant's* David Fink asked Bush what he and his father talked about when they weren't talking politics.

"Sexual harassment on the job is not a problem for virtuous women."

—Phyllis Schlafly, founder of the Eagle Forum, 2001.

"She's the lump in the bed next to me."

—President George W. Bush, referring to his wife, Laura, during a July 2003 press conference.

"Hillary Clinton is like some hellish housewife who has seen something that she really, really wants and won't stop nagging you until you finally say, fine, take it, be the damn president, just leave me alone."

—Leon Wieseltier, literary editor of *The New Republic*, October, 2007.

"If we took away women's right to vote, we'd never have to worry about another Democratic president. It's kind of a pipe dream; it's a personal fantasy of mine."

—Ann Coulter, June, 2008.

Social Programs

"We want one class of persons to have a liberal education, and we want another class of persons, a very much larger class of necessity in every society, to forego the privilege of a liberal education and fit themselves to perform specific difficult manual tasks."

—President Woodrow Wilson, 1915.

"It is better for all the world if instead of waiting to execute degenerate offspring for crime or to let them starve for their imbecility, society can prevent those who are manifestly unfit from continuing their kind."

—Supreme Court Justice Oliver Wendell Holmes, in his majority opinion in the case of *Buck v. Bell,* 1927. In this case, the U.S. Supreme Court upheld as constitutional a Virginia statute instituting compulsory sterilization of the mentally retarded "for the protection and health of the state."

"Many persons left their jobs for the more profitable one of selling apples."

—President Herbert Hoover, 1932.

"The State of California has no business subsidizing intellectual curiosity."

—Ronald Reagan, while governor of California, 1968.

"Oh, I've got too many of those now to hire you."

—Virginia Senator William Scott, after a prospective staff member told him she was Jewish, 1976.

"The poor don't need gas because they're not working."

"The elderly eat less."

—S. I. Hayakawa, senator from California,
explaining why the elderly don't need special support or food-stamp eligibility, 1979.

"Old people have a duty to die and get out of the way."

—Richard Lamm, governor of Colorado, 1981.

"Your tax dollars are being used to pay for grade-school classes that teach our children that cannibalism, wife-swapping, and the murder of infants and the elderly are acceptable behavior."

—Senator Jesse Helms of North Carolina, in a 1981 fund-raising letter for the National Conservative Political Action Committee.

"We have every mixture you can have. I have a black, I have a woman, two Jews, and a cripple."

—James Watt, Secretary of the Interior in the Reagan administration, describing an Interior Department Advisory Group, 1982.

"What we have found in this country, and maybe we're more aware of it now, is one problem that we've had, even in the best of times, and that is the people who are sleeping on the grates, the homeless, who are homeless, you might say, by choice."

—President Ronald Reagan, 1984.

"You haven't thought about a new husband, have you?"

—Texas Senator Phil Gramm, responding to an elderly African American widow who complained that Gramm's proposals to cut Social Security and Medicare benefits would make it difficult for her to remain independent, 1986.

"We're the only nation in the world where all of our poor people are fat."

—Texas Senator Phil Gramm, 1988.

"The standard of living of the average American has to decline."

—Federal Reserve Chairman Paul Volcker, 1989.

"We didn't do too well with the animal vote, did we? Isn't it the animals who live there in those projects?"

—New York Senator Al D'Amato, explaining why he refused to help find funding for a low-income housing project in Brooklyn, 1991.

"I stay out of their way at K-Mart."

—Willie Brown, mayor of San Francisco, when he was asked what he does to help the poor, 1996.

"The welfare state kills more people in a year than private business."

—Speaker of the House Newt Gingrich, 1997.

"I don't understand how poor people think."

—President-elect George W. Bush, December 2000.

"If Americans are serious about making major inroads on illegitimacy, the most important unanswered policy question is this: what would be the effect of eliminating welfare for unmarried mothers altogether? . . . A plausible test case would be for a state with a relatively small caseload and a history of effective nongovernmental social welfare . . . to cut off all benefits for girls under the age of 21."

—Charles Murray, in a Brookings Institution volume entitled *The New World of Welfare*, 2001.

"No president has done more for human rights than I have."

—President George W. Bush, in a remark to *New Yorker* writer Ken Auletta, quoted in the *New York Times*, January 20, 2004.

"I'd rather see my children infected with a sexually transmitted disease than know there was such a thing as a condom."

—Phyllis Schlafly, 2004.

"What I'm hearing, which is sort of scary, is they all want to stay in Texas. Everyone is so overwhelmed by the hospitality. And so many of the people in here, you know, were underprivileged anyway, so this is working very well for them."

—Barbara Bush, while visiting Katrina evacuees in the Houston Astrodome, September 6, 2005.

"We finally cleaned up public housing in New Orleans. We couldn't do it, but God did it."

—Richard Baker, representative from New Orleans, speaking to a group of lobbyists, September 2005.

"Where did this idea come from that everybody deserves a free education? Free medical care? Free whatever? It comes from Moscow. From Russia. It comes straight out of the pit of hell."

—Debbie Riddle, Texas state representative, October, 2005.

"Because of the facts, and the lack of my comprehensive assessment of the risks and benefits of greenhouse gas emissions and regulation, it is simply impossible to conclude that the net effect of greenhouse gases is an endangerment of health and welfare."

—Amicus brief submitted by the Competitive Enterprise Institute in *Commonwealth of Massachusetts v. U.S. Environmental Protection Agency*, 2006.

"People have access to health care in America. After all, you just go to an emergency room."

—President George W. Bush, when asked about the fact that millions of Americans have no health insurance, July 2006.

"I don't know about you, but I don't remember ever asking how much something was going to cost when it came to health care."

—President George W. Bush, responding to a question about universal health care before an audience in Chattanooga, Tennessee, February 2007.

God and Religion

"What is it the Bible teaches us? Rapine, cruelty, and murder. What is it the [New] Testament teaches us? To believe that the Almighty committed debauchery with a woman engaged to be married. Of all the systems of religion that ever were invented, there is none more derogatory to the Almighty, more unedifying to man, more repugnant to reason, and more contradictory in itself than this thing called Christianity."

—Thomas Paine in *The Age of Reason*, 1795.

"All the ills from which America suffers can be traced back to the teaching of evolution. It would be better to destroy every other book ever written and save just the first three verses of Genesis."

—William Jennings Bryan, Democratic presidential candidate, 1924.

"For us there are two sorts of people in the world. There are those who are Christians and support free enterprise, and then there are the others."

—Secretary of State John Foster Dulles, 1954.

"He [the Holy Ghost] comes and speaks to me about two in the morning, when I have to give the word to the boys, and I get the word from God whether to bomb or not."

—President Lyndon B. Johnson to Austrian ambassador Ernst Lemberger, 1966.

"The evangelical Christians are cockroaches coming out from the baseboards of the Bible Belt."

—Neil Bush, in a speech for his father, George H. W. Bush, in Iowa, 1988.

"AIDS is the wrath of a just God against homosexuals."

—Reverend Jerry Falwell, February 1993.

"Just like what Nazi Germany did to the Jews, so liberal America is now doing to the evangelical Christians. It's no different. It is the same thing. It is the Democratic congress, the liberal-based media, and the homosexuals who want to destroy the Christians."

—Reverend Pat Robertson, 1994.

"I feel like God wants me to run for president. I can't explain it, but I sense my country's going to need me. Something is going to happen. I know it won't be easy for me or my family, but God wants me to do it."

—George W. Bush, speaking to Texas evangelical leader James Robinson, spring 2000.

"What we saw on Tuesday, as terrible as it is, could be miniscule if, in fact, God continues to lift the curtain and allow the enemies of America to give us probably what we deserve. The ACLU had to take a lot of blame for this. Throwing God out of the public square, out of the schools. The abortionists have got to bear some burden for this because God will not be mocked. . . . I really believe that the pagans and the abortionists and the feminists and the gays and the lesbians . . . the ACLU, People for the American Way, all of them who try to secularize America . . . I point the finger in their face and say you helped this happen."

—Reverend Jerry Falwell, September 13, 2001, referring to the terrorist attack of 9/11.

"We should invade Muslim countries, kill their leaders, and convert them to Christianity."

—Ann Coulter, in the *National Review*, September 13, 2001.

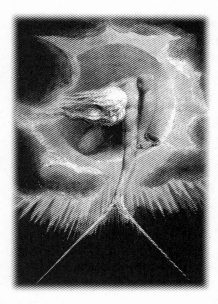

"The god of Islam is not the same god. He's not the son of God of the Christian or Judeo-Christian faith. It's a different god, and I believe it's a very evil and wicked religion."

—Reverend Franklin Graham, son of Reverend Billy Graham, September 2002.

"The prophet Muhammad was a demon-obsessed pedophile."

—Reverend Jerry Vines, former head of the Southern Baptist Convention (SBC), September 2002. The day after Vines's comment was in the news, President Bush praised the SBC for its "religious tolerance."

"I knew my God was bigger than his. I knew that my God was real and his was an idol. . . . Why do they hate us? The answer to that is because we're a Christian nation. We are hated because we are a nation of believers. . . . Our spiritual enemy will only be defeated if we come against them in the name of Jesus. . . . George Bush was not elected by a majority of the voters in the United States, he was appointed by God."

—Lieutenant General William G. "Jerry" Boykin, speaking to a church audience in Oregon, June 2003, about his battles with warlords in Somalia in 1993, and about the "War on Terror." Rather than being reprimanded for his inflammatory comments, he was promoted to the position of Deputy Undersecretary of Defense for Intelligence.

"I'm driven with a mission from God. He told me, 'George, go and fight those terrorists in Afghanistan,' and I struck them. And he told me, 'George, go and end the tyranny in Iraq,' and I did. And now I am determined to solve the problem in the Middle East."

—President George W. Bush, to Palestinian foreign minister Abu Mazen, June 2003.

"The enemy has got a face. He's called Satan. He's in Fallujah and we're going to destroy him."

—U.S. Marine Colonel Gary Brandl, November 2004.

"God is pro-war."

—Reverend Jerry Falwell, November 2004.

"For the believing Christian, death is no big deal."

—Supreme Court Justice Antonin Scalia, while speaking on the subject of the death penalty at the University of Chicago Divinity School, May 2005.

"Global environmental annihilation is a divine requirement for Christ's return."

—A member of the Christian Four-Wheelers, quoted in *Divine Destruction*, 2005.

"In my belief, God judged New Orleans for the sin of shedding innocent blood through abortion."

—South Carolina anti-abortion activist Steve Lefemine, September 2005.

"The day Bourbon Street and the French Quarter was flooded was the day that 125,000 homosexuals were going to be celebrating sin in the streets. . . . We're calling it an act of God."

—Michael Marcavage, head of Repent America, speaking of the devastation caused by Hurricane Katrina, September 2005.

U.S. Intelligence Agencies
and Covert Operations

"He's on our side now, that's all that matters."

—OSS Officer Allen Dulles, 1946, regarding questions about why U.S.
intelligence was employing Reinhard Gehlen, who had been the head
of Hitler's espionage operations in eastern Europe and the USSR
during World War II.

"The CIA should carry out rumor-spreading, bribery, the organization of non-communist fronts, guerrilla movements, underground armies, sabotage, and assassination."

—National Security Council Report, June 1948.

"[He's] a likeable rogue who hasn't, to my certain knowledge, ever bowed down to a graven image. He has, however, committed sacrilege, blasphemy, murder, adultery, and theft."

—Miles Copeland, CIA station chief in Damascus, Syria, June 1949,
referring to Colonel Adib Shishakli, who the CIA had just installed as
Syria's new leader.

"The fact that [CIA Director] Allen [Dulles] knew about the assassination plot and did not forbid it would have been a circumlocutious matter. What is very difficult for anybody to understand is that if you say, in however veiled or murky terms, that you are going to do something, and if the terms aren't so murky that the listener doesn't know what you're going to do, and if you don't receive a negative, and you think it will advance the cause, you go ahead and do it. And so you were never explicitly authorized, but you have to add that the whole system was set up so the Chief of State doesn't have to authorize things explicitly."

—Richard Bissell, CIA deputy director of plans, 1960.

"Getting rid of Castro is the top priority in the U.S. Government—all else is secondary. No time, money, effort, or manpower is to be spared. The final chapter on Cuba has not been written."

—Attorney General Robert F. Kennedy, 1961. After the failed Bay of Pigs invasion of Cuba in April 1961, the Kennedy administration launched Operation Mongoose, a top-secret program of terror on the Castro regime to attempt to drive him from power. Mongoose included ZR/RIFLE, the secret program to assassinate Castro.

"Bobby Kennedy was running it—hour by hour. We were conducting two raids a week at the height of that program against mainland Cuba. People were being killed, sugar mills were blown up, and bridges were demolished. We were using fast boats and mother ships, and the U.S. Army was supporting and training these forces."

—General Alexander Haig, in a 1997 interview, referring to Operation Mongoose.

"Recruit and deploy the Catholic Church and the Cuban underworld against Castro, fracture the regime from within, sabotage the economy, subvert the secret police, destroy the crops with biological or chemical warfare, and change the regime before the next congressional elections in November."

—Brigadier General Ed Lansdale, in a 1962 memo to Attorney General Robert Kennedy, outlining his ideas on how to overthrow Fidel Castro.

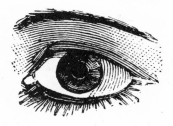

"The outfit [the Mafia] and the CIA are sides of the same coin. Sometimes our government can't do shit on the up-and-up. Sometimes they need a little trouble somewhere or maybe they need some bastard taken care of . . . they can't get caught doing shit like that . . . but we can. Guns, a hit, muscle . . . whatever dirty work needs to be done. . . . We're on the same side, we're working for the same things."

—Sam Giancana, Mafia boss of Chicago, 1966.

"I want it implemented! Goddammit, get in and get those files. Blow the safe and get it."

—President Richard M. Nixon, to White House Chief of Staff H.R. Haldeman, referring to a plan to get information on Daniel Ellsberg, after he had leaked *The Pentagon Papers* to the media, from his psychiatrist's office, June 1971.

"[The U.S. secret bombing in Laos] was something of which we can be proud as Americans. It has involved virtually no American casualties. What we are getting for our money there is, I think, to use the old phrase, very cost-effective."

—Undersecretary of State Alexis Johnson, July 1971, reporting to a Senate committee hearing on the "secret" war in Laos from 1965-1973. During that period, in what was named Operation Hardnose, nearly two million tons of bombs poured down on the defenseless people of Laos. In 1962 there were some 750,000 Hmong living in Laos. By 1975 only about 10,000 remained.

"They are trained, for example, to confront disorders and student demonstrations, to prepare dossiers, to make the best possible use of bank data and tax returns of individuals, etc. In other words, to watch over the population of their country with the means offered by technology. This is what I call techno-fascism."

—Former CIA agent Victor Marchetti, speaking of the training provided by the CIA to the Italian security services, 1974.

"We are the Praetorian Guard. It's our job to protect the president. We work for the president . . . and then he goes to the American public. We're the fall guys. We take the blame and that's the way it works."

—Sam Halpern, who assisted in Operation Mongoose, the Kennedy administration's secret Cuban sabotage operation of the early 1960s, in testimony before senate hearings, 1975.

"It's one of the things that I think probably irritates me more than any of the allegations against the Agency, and that is that we were involved in the drug traffic at any time. . . . We never were! After all, the people who ran the Agency, the people who worked in various places on the operational side all over the world, were perfectly decent Americans."

—Former CIA Director Richard Helms, after congressional hearings in 1975 revealed that the CIA had been deeply involved in the worldwide drug trade since the end of World War II.

"Covert action should not be confused with missionary work."

—Secretary of State Henry Kissinger, testifying in 1975 before the House Select Committee on Intelligence Activities regarding the fact that the United States had merely stood by while Iraqi troops carried out a horrible massacre of thousands of Kurds. The Kurds had been promised by both Kissinger and President Nixon that they would receive protection from the United States if they revolted.

"We're not going to let a little thing like drugs get in the way of the political situation."

—Reagan administration official, responding in a top-secret 1983 memo to the accusation that the Afghan rebels were using raw opium as payment for shipments of weapons and supplies, which the CIA was then selling to drug agents in Pakistan, who in turn refined it into heroin. The Drug Enforcement Administration was estimating that at the time, 70 percent of the world's high-grade heroin originated in Pakistan.

"It is possible to neutralize carefully selected and planned targets, such as court judges, police and state security officials, etc. For psychological purposes it is necessary to take extreme precautions. . . . The mission to replace the individual should be followed by extensive explanation of the reason why it was necessary for the good of the people."

—1984 Contra-era CIA training manual titled *Psychological Operations in Guerrilla Warfare.*

"Americans will never make concessions to terrorists—to do so would only invite more terrorism. . . . Once we head down that path there would be no end to it, no end to the suffering of innocent people, no end to the bloody ransom all civilized people must pay."

—President Ronald Reagan, 1985. At that time, however, the Reagan Administration was secretly and illegally selling arms to Iran to help fund its covert operations with the Contra forces in Nicaragua, in spite of the fact that in January 1984 the U.S. State Department had officially declared Iran to be "a sponsor of international terrorism."

"Fuck the Congress. If it weren't for those liberals in Congress, we wouldn't be doing half of what we do illegally."

—Lieutenant Colonel Oliver North, 1985. North was in charge of the illegal, secret operation to supply the Contra rebels in Nicaragua.

"You were giving arms to people who were going to go out and get ground up in battle. Now it seems they will use the same weapons to kill each other. It's one of those undesirable spin-offs."

—Stansfield Turner, CIA director during the Carter administration, commenting on the CIA's having secretly sold billions of dollars worth of weapons to the Afghan rebels in their struggle against the Soviet Union during the 1980s. After the Soviets pulled out in 1988, the rebels we had supplied then turned on each other in a bloody civil war in which over a million civilians were killed.

"Our main mission was to do as much damage as possible to the Soviets. We didn't really have the resources or the time to devote to an investigation of the drug trade. . . . I don't think we need to apologize for this. Every situation has its fallout. . . . There was fallout in terms of drugs, yes. But the main objective was accomplished. The Soviets left Afghanistan."

—Charles Cogan, former director of the CIA's secret Afghanistan operation during the 1980s. During the 1980s, Afghanistan supplied 60 percent of the demand for heroin in the United States, and the CIA was funding its secret operations with the profits from the heroin trade.

"It would be an embarrassing situation if you ever had a roll call of everybody in the Guatemalan Army who ever collected a CIA paycheck."

—Colonel George Hooker, 1990. Hooker was the head of the U.S. Defense Intelligence Agency in Guatemala from 1985 to 1989.

"You don't want to be in a position of dealing with military officials or officials in that government who are known by everyone to have blood on their hands unless there is a legitimate intelligence goal to be served. If a person is notorious for butchering people, breaking the law, then the fact that the CIA is in contact with that individual has to be balanced against the information that individual is likely to provide."

—Fred Hitz, inspector general of the CIA, April 1995.

Truth and Propaganda

"Il Duce is a very upstanding chap and has done a great job in Italy."

—Thomas Lamont, partner in J.P. Morgan, 1922.

"That remarkable man, Benito Mussolini, should be praised for bringing a spirit of order, discipline, hard work, patriotic devotion, and faith."

—Otto Kahn, of Kuhn, Loeb, & Co, 1922. During the first five months of 1921, Mussolini's fascist forces had gone on a rampage, ransacking over 100 labor organizations' headquarters, murdering close to 200 workers, and injuring over 1,000 others in crushing workers' strikes. Over 2,300 workers had been arrested and thrown in jail.

"If we understand the mechanisms and motives of the group mind, is it not possible to control and regiment the masses according to our will without their knowing? The recent practice of propaganda has proved that is possible."

—Edward Bernays, considered the "Father of Public Relations," 1938.

"In spite of the risk involved in letting the Japanese fire the first shot, we realized that in order to have the full support of the American people, it was desirable to make sure the Japanese were the ones to do this so that there should remain no doubt in anyone's mind as to who were the aggressors."

—Henry Stimson, secretary of war, in his diary, October 1941.

"All procedures should be treated as routine in order to minimize any adverse publicity."

—U.S. Navy memo of 1946, to those in charge of decontamination operations in San Francisco Bay of ships that had been used as part of Operation Crossroads at Bikini Atoll in the Pacific. At Bikini two atomic bombs were detonated over a fleet of 100 warships. Several of the ships, "hot" with radioactivity, were towed to San Francisco to be "cleaned off," resulting in huge amounts of radioactive materials being dumped into the bay.

"Americans must be prepared physically, mentally, and morally to drop atom bombs on Russia at the first sign of aggression. Our people must be conditioned to accept this type of retaliation."

—Lieutenant General Jimmy Doolittle, 1947.

"Mr. President, the only way you are ever going to get this is to make a speech and scare the hell out of the country."

—Arthur Vandenberg, chairman of the Senate Foreign Relations Committee, to President Harry Truman, regarding getting an open-ended commitment to assert U.S. control over the eastern Mediterranean, across Asia Minor, and deep into the Persian Gulf, October 1947.

"I think that, however much we whip up sentiment, we are going to run into vast opposition among informed people to a huge arms race. We will be warned that we are heading toward a 'garrison state.' Moreover, even if we should sell the idea, I fear that the U.S. public would rapidly tire of such an effort. In the absence of real and continuing crises . . . [the U.S. public can] be sold and be kept sold on a massive program of developing new weapons [by] creating a permanent crisis atmosphere—a centrally coordinated Cold War."

— "Eyes Only" memo to Secretary of State Dean Acheson from Edward W. Barrett, assistant secretary of state for Public Affairs, chair of the Interdepartmental Psychological Strategy Board, and head of the Truman administration's "Campaign of Truth," 1958.

"It is not in the public interest that any of the conversations or communications of executive branch personnel or any documents concerning such advice be disclosed."

—President Dwight D. Eisenhower, October 1954.

"The Department has no evidence that indicates this is anything other than a revolt of Guatemalans against the government."

—Secretary of State John Foster Dulles, in a statement to the press regarding the overthrow of the democratically elected government of Guatemala in 1954. In fact, however, the Eisenhower administration had instigated, planned, and carried out the whole revolt.

"Are the American people entitled to know whether we are intervening in Cuba or intend to do so in the future? The answer to that question is no."

—Secretary of State Dean Rusk, three days before the U.S. invasion of Cuba at the Bay of Pigs, April 1961.

Q: "Well, what do you make, General, of the principle of the people's right to know?"

A: "I don't believe in that as a general principle."

—General Maxwell D. Taylor, President John F. Kennedy's chairman of the Joint Chiefs of Staff, 1962.

"[Create] incidents around Guantanamo . . . to give the genuine appearance of being done by hostile Cuban forces."

"[Create] the appearance of an attack on Guantanamo. We could blow up a U.S. ship or paint an F-86 to look like a Cuban MIG-type aircraft and have it destroy a U.S. drone aircraft."

"Using the MIG mock-up to shoot down a U.S. charter airline drone that would then be reported to have had U.S. college students aboard."

—From documents released in 1997, suggesting ideas for a "Pretext for Invasion," part of OPLAN 314, created in April 1962 to plan for a second invasion of Cuba.

"There are those that say you ought to go north and drop bombs, to try to wipe out the supply lines. . . . We don't want our American boys to do the fighting for Asian boys. We don't want to get involved in a nation with 700 million people and get tied down in a land war in Asia."

"But we are not about to send American boys nine or ten thousand miles away from home to do what Asian boys ought to be doing for themselves."

—President Lyndon Johnson, during the 1964 presidential campaign.

"Anything damaging to the image of the American president should be suppressed to protect the younger generation."

—Judge Edward Ruzzo, June 1964. Ruzzo was referring to the possible publication of former President Warren G. Harding's embarrassing love letters to a married woman.

"I wouldn't think he would tell it under oath, no . . . he ought not to tell it under oath. Maybe not tell it to his own government."

—Allen Dulles, former CIA director, explaining to his fellow Warren Commission members about how CIA agents operated in terms of secrets, 1964.

"Hell, those damn stupid sailors were just shooting at flying fish."

—President Lyndon B. Johnson, 1968, referring to the Gulf of Tonkin incident in August 1964 when U.S. ships were alleged to have been attacked by North Vietnamese PT boats. Johnson had used the bogus attack to get permission from Congress to widen the war in Vietnam.

"Without censorship, things can get terribly confused in the public mind."

—General William Westmoreland, August 1964.

"It was not a bombing of Cambodia. It was a bombing of North Vietnam in Cambodia."

—National Security Advisor Henry Kissinger, responding to media questions regarding the Nixon administration's secret bombing of Cambodia, 1970.

"There was a pretty general consensus that more interviews with these subjects are in order for plenty of reasons, chief of which are it will enhance the paranoia endemic in these circles and will further serve to get the point across that there is an FBI agent behind every mailbox."

—Internal FBI memo regarding harassment of "New Left" political activists in the United States, 1970.

"That's exactly what I expect. Look, if you think any American official is going to tell you the truth, then you're stupid."

—Arthur Sylvester, assistant secretary of Defense for Public Affairs in the Nixon administration, 1971. Sylvester had told U.S. newsmen that it was their duty to only write stories that cast the United States in a positive light when one of the reporters questioned him by saying, "Surely, Arthur, you don't expect the American press to be handmaidens of the government."

"One day we'll get them [the leakers] to the ground where we want them. And we'll stick our heels in, step on them hard, and twist. Step on them, crush them, show them no mercy."

—President Richard M. Nixon to Henry Kissinger onboard the presidential yacht, *Sequoia,* June 1971, after the leak of the *Pentagon Papers* to the media.

"The CIA had nothing to do with the [Chilean] coup, to the best of my knowledge and belief."

—Secretary of State Henry Kissinger, September 1973. It's known now, of course, that the United States was fully behind the coup.

"The Central Intelligence Agency owns everyone of any significance in the major media."

—Former CIA Director William Colby, 1975.

"The First Amendment is only an amendment."

—Ray S. Cline, deputy director of the CIA, testifying to Congress regarding the CIA's secret links to the media, 1975.

"We did often lie, mislead, deceive, try to use [the press], and to con them."

—Ray Price, lead speechwriter for Richard Nixon, in a 1976 interview.

"I was not lying. I said things that later on seemed to be untrue."

"Well, when the president does it, it is not illegal."

—Richard Nixon, in his interviews with David Frost, 1977.

"Here's the Constitution, you show me anywhere in there about the public's right to know, that you have a right to answers to questions. It ain't there."

—Lyn Nofziger, Ronald Reagan's 1980 campaign press secretary.

"I very frankly think that they've been getting a bad deal."

—President Ronald Reagan in 1983, referring to media treatment of the government of General Efraim Rios Montt in Guatemala. Amnesty International had just released a report revealing that 2,600 Indians and peasants had been slaughtered during the period from July 1982 to March 1983.

"Controlling minds is more important than controlling territory. The only territory you want to hold is the six inches between the ears of the peasant."

—Colonel John Waghelstein, chief of the U.S. Military Advisory Group in El Salvador, 1983.

"I think the most critical special operations mission we have today is to persuade the American people that the communists are out to get us. If we can win this war of ideas, we can win everywhere else."

—J. Michael Kelly, deputy assistant secretary of the U.S. Air Force, 1985.

"Our most pressing problem is not in the third world, but here at home in the struggle for the minds of people."

—George Tanham, vice president of the Rand Corporation, 1985.

"The idea is to slowly demonize the Sandinista government in order to turn it into a real enemy in the minds of the American people, thereby eroding their resistance to U.S. support for the contras and, perhaps, to a future military intervention in the region."

—Quote from a "Reagan administration official" regarding Oliver North's propaganda operation, cited in Knight-Ridder newspapers, August 1985.

"I was out of the loop."

—Vice President George H. W. Bush, on numerous occasions, describing his role in the Iran-Contra guns-for-hostages operation.

"On the news at this time is the question of the hostages. I'm one of the few people that know fully the details. . . . This is one operation that had been held very, very tight, and I hope it will not leak."

—Vice President George H. W. Bush, in a recording in his taped diary, November 5, 1986.

"We did not—repeat, did not—trade weapons or anything else for hostages."

—President Ronald Reagan, in a speech to the nation on November 13, 1986, regarding the Iran-Contra scandal that had erupted. At the time, of course, the Reagan administration was deeply involved in secretly selling weapons to Iran to fund the Contra forces in Nicaragua.

"I preach a good line, but I practice what most people in my profession practice. Once in a while, I like to think that I get a little bit further down the road, but so do other reporters. As a rule, we are, if not handmaidens of the establishment, at least blood brothers to the establishment. . . . We end up the day usually having some version of what the White House . . . has suggested as a story."

—Sam Donaldson of ABC News, 1987.

"We will get nowhere without first stipulating that, while circumstances alter almost any case you can think of, the president has an inherent right—perhaps an obligation in particular situations—to deceive."

—Philip L Geyelin, editor of the *Washington Post's* editorial page, 1987.

"You do not lie to Congress. You don't lie—you put your own interpretation of what the truth is."

—Robert C. McFarlane, National Security advisor for Ronald Reagan, 1988.

"I will never apologize for the United States—I don't care what the facts are."

—Vice President George H. W. Bush, explaining his position on the downing of an Iranian commercial airliner, 1988. For the record, the plane was on a routine flight in a commercial corridor in Iranian airspace, and the targeting of it by U.S. forces was blatantly illegal.

"From Mexico to Argentina, Latin American governments today roundly condemned the use of force by the United States against General Manuel Antonio Noriega of Panama."

—News report on December 20, 1989, the day of the U.S. invasion of Panama, called "Operation Just Cause" by the George H. W. Bush administration. The Organization of American States (OAS) passed a resolution by a vote of 20 to 1 condemning the invasion as a "gross violation of international law." The only OAS member to vote against the resolution was the United States.

"I appreciate the support that we've received, strong support, from our Latin American neighbors."

—President George H. W. Bush, December 21, 1989.

"We live in a dirty and dangerous world. There are some things the general public does not need to know and shouldn't. I believe democracy flourishes when the government can take legitimate steps to keep its secrets and when the press can decide whether to print what it knows."

—Katherine Graham, owner of the *Washington Post*, in a speech given at CIA headquarters, January 1990.

"We have no opinion on . . . your border disagreement with Kuwait. . . . The issue is not associated with America."

—James Baker III, secretary of state to President George H. W. Bush in a diplomatic message to Saddam Hussein, July 5, 1990.

"We do not have any defense treaties with Kuwait, and there are no special defense or security commitments to Kuwait."

—U.S. State Department spokesperson Margaret Tutwiler to the press, July 24, 1990.

"The U.S. has no opinion on Arab–Arab conflicts like your border disagreement with Kuwait."

—U.S. Ambassador to Iraq April Glaspie, to Saddam Hussein, July 25, 1990.

"The U.S. has no defense relationship with any Gulf country. This is clear. We have historically avoided taking positions on border disputes. . . . It would be correct to say that we do not have a treaty commitment which would obligate us to engage U.S. forces in Kuwait."

—Assistant Secretary of State John Kelly, to the House Subcommittee on Foreign Affairs, July 31, 1990. On August 2, 1990, Iraqi forces invaded Kuwait and President Bush announced that the United States would invade if Saddam Hussein refused to withdraw his troops.

"I think one of the greatest problems we have in the Republican Party is that we don't encourage you to be nasty. We are engaged in reshaping the whole nation through the news media."

—Speaker of the House Newt Gingrich, 1995.

"Are you going to tell kids that Thomas Jefferson didn't believe in Jesus?"

—A textbook editor to author James W. Loewen, 1998.

[The war on terror] will not end until every terrorist group of global reach has been found, stopped, and defeated."

"We will direct every resource at our command . . . to the disruption and to the defeat of the global terrorist network."

"Our nation . . . will lift a dark threat of violence from our people and our future. We will rally the world to this cause by our efforts, by our courage. We will not tire, we will not falter, and we will not fail."

—President George W. Bush, in his address to a Joint Session of Congress, September 21, 2001.

"I don't think you can win it. But I think you can create conditions so that those who use terror as a tool are less acceptable in parts of the world, let's put it that way."

—President George W. Bush, in an interview with NBC's Matt Lauer, October 2004.

"Let's keep in mind the fact that this war's going to happen regardless of what [the source] said or didn't say, and the Powers That Be probably aren't terribly interested in whether [the source] knows what he's talking about."

—CIA official to Secretary of State Colin Powell, prior to his United Nations speech February, 2002. Another CIA official had just informed Powell that "the source" of information Powell was using couldn't be relied upon as truthful.

"I'd rather have them [American troops] sacrificing on behalf of our nation than, you know, endless hours of testimony on congressional hill."

—President George W. Bush to the National Security Agency, May 2002.

"They're [the Iraqis] going to welcome us. It'll be like the American army going through the streets of Paris. They're sitting there ready to form a new government. The people will be so happy with their freedoms that we'll probably back ourselves out of there within a month or two."

—Vice President Dick Cheney, September 2002.

"From a marketing point of view, you don't introduce new products in August."

—Andrew Card, White House Chief of Staff, explaining on September 7, 2002, why the Bush administration's coordinated effort to convince the world of the urgent danger presented by Saddam Hussein's weapons of mass destruction had to wait until after Labor Day.

"The sooner the fighting begins in Iraq, the nearer we are to its imminent end. Which means, in other words, this 'rush to war' should really be seen as the ultimate 'rush to peace.'"

—David Frum, former White House speechwriter, February 24, 2003.

"Why should we hear about body bags and deaths and how many, what day it's gonna happen? It's not relevant. So why should I waste my beautiful mind on something like that?"

—Barbara Bush, in an interview with Diane Sawyer of ABC News, March 2003.

"We found the weapons of mass destruction, and those who said otherwise were wrong."

—President George W. Bush, in an interview with Polish television, May 29, 2003. Bush obviously never repeated that story.

"You're good stewards of the quality of the air."

—President George W. Bush, at the Detroit Edison power plant in Monroe, Michigan in September 2003. In 2001, the plant sent 102,700 tons of sulfur dioxide, 45,900 tons of nitrogen oxide, 810 pounds of mercury, and 17.6 million tons of carbon dioxide into the air.

"I wish you would have given me this written question ahead of time, so I could plan for it. I'm sure something will pop into my head here in the midst of this press conference, with all the pressure of trying to come up with an answer, but it hasn't yet. I just haven't—you just put me under the spot here and maybe I'm not as quick on my feet as I should be in coming up with one."

—President George W. Bush, at an April 13, 2004, press conference, after a member of the White House press corps asked the president to name a mistake he'd made while in office.

"There was nothing in the Presidential Daily Briefing document of August 6, 2001, that suggested there was going to be a threat to the United States."

—National Security Advisor Condoleezza Rice, testifying before the 9/11 Commission, April 8, 2004. The title of that briefing document, however, was, "Bin Laden Determined to Attack Inside the U.S."

"The government asking the press not to report Abu Ghraib is not against our principles. It is not suppression of the news."

—Secretary of Defense Donald Rumsfeld, in senate testimony regarding prisoner abuse at Abu Ghraib, Iraq, May 2004.

"[You're] in what we call the reality-based community, people who believe that solutions emerge from your judicious study of discernible reality. That's not the way the world really works any more. We're an empire now, and when we act, we create our own reality. And while you're studying that reality—judiciously, as you will—we'll act again, creating other new realities, which you can study too, and that's how things will sort out. We're history's actors . . . and you, all of you, will be left to just study what we do."

—Karl Rove, in an interview with writer Ron Suskind, published in the *New York Times Magazine*, October 17, 2004.

"In my line of work you got to keep repeating things over and over and over again for the truth to sink in, to kind of catapult the propaganda."

—President George W. Bush, May 2005.

"The prisoners are well treated in Guantanamo. There's total transparency. . . . And you're welcome to go. The press, of course, is welcome to go down to Guantanamo. . . . And for those of you who have doubt, I'd suggest buying an airplane ticket and going down and look—take a look for yourself."

—President George W. Bush, at a press appearance in Lyngby, Denmark, July 6, 2005. CNN, taking Bush up on his invitation to visit the Guantanamo Bay military prison in Cuba, took a camera crew to Guantanamo the very next day, but they were denied access to portions of the base, and the video they were able to shoot was censored.

"I don't think anybody anticipated the breach of the levees."

—President George W. Bush, September 1, 2005, two days after hurricane Katrina hit New Orleans. In fact, on the day before Katrina slammed into New Orleans, federal disaster officials had warned the president specifically about the levees in a videotaped meeting later obtained by the Associated Press.

"If the president wants to go to war, our job is to find the intelligence to allow him to do so."

—Alan Foley, director of CIA Weapons Intelligence, Nonproliferation and Arms Control Center, quoted in *The Italian Letter*, April 2007.

Death Squads, Torture, and Assassination

"I want no prisoners. I wish you to kill and burn. The more you kill and the more you burn, the better you will please me."

—Colonel Jacob Smith, September 1901, giving orders to his troops in crushing the Filipino rebellion of 1901–1902. Smith had taken part in the Wounded Knee massacre in the Dakota Territory a decade earlier.

"We had a hard time catching him because no matter how much we tortured, we could never get people to inform."

"I shot a guy at the polls, and took part in rapes, burning huts, and cutting off genitals. I had nightmares for years. I didn't have much of a conscience while I was in the Marines. We were taught not to have a conscience."

—Former U.S. Marine Bill Gandall, who spent two years in the late 1920s helping a Nicaraguan dictatorship fight rebel leader Augusto César Sandino and his freedom forces.

"This is certainly the most toxic inorganic element, and it produces a particular fibrotic tumor at the site of local application. The amount necessary to produce these tumors is a few micrograms."

—1952 CIA memo reporting on the carcinogenic effects of beryllium. The CIA had created compounds that could cause virulent cancers in victims and not be detected in autopsies.

"No assassination instruction should ever be written or recorded. . . . The simplest tools are often the most efficient means of assassination . . . anything hard, heavy, and handy will suffice. . . . The most efficient accident is a fall of 75 feet or more onto a hard surface. Falls before trains and subway cars are usually effective, but require exact timing. . . . Assassinations can seldom be employed with a clear conscience. Persons who are morally squeamish should not attempt it."

—CIA training manual, 1954.

"We all got together and got a goddamn bunch of thugs and we went in and assassinated him."

—President Lyndon Johnson, October 1967, referring to the U.S. government's plot to overthrow President Ngo Dinh Diem of South Vietnam in November 1963.

"The principle coercive techniques are arrest, detention, the deprivation of sensory stimuli, threats and fear, debility, pain, heightened suggestibility and hypnosis, and drugs. The interrogatee's defenses crumble, and he becomes more childlike."

"Interrogations conducted under compulsion or duress are especially likely to involve illegality. Therefore, prior headquarters approval must be obtained for the interrogation of any source: one, if bodily harm is to be inflicted; two, if medical, chemical, or electrical methods are to be used; three [deleted]."

—Excerpts from *Kubarc Counterintelligence Interrogation*, a secret 1963 CIA handbook for dealing with spies, defectors, and suspected double agents, written by Jesus Angleton, the CIA's Chief of Counterintelligence in the 1950s and 1960s. "Kubarc" is an agency code word.

"I say get 'em by the balls, and their hearts and minds will follow."

—Mendel Rivers, representative from South Carolina, 1968.

"No! We've got to have more of this. Assassinations. Killings. That's what they're [the communists] doing."

—President Richard M. Nixon, 1969.

"The precise pain in the precise place, at the precise time. You must be careful, you should avoid excesses. . . . When you get what you want, and I always get it, it may be good to prolong the session a little to apply another softening up. Not to extract information now, but only as a political measure, to create a healthy fear of meddling in subversive activities."

—Dan Mitrione, 1970. Mitrione had been sent to Uruguay by the U.S. Office of Public Safety to teach torture techniques to the Uruguayan police forces.

"It was a sterile, depersonalized murder program. It was completely indiscriminate."

—A former CIA agent, speaking on condition of anonymity in 1972 about the CIA's Operation Phoenix, in which approximately 40,000 South Vietnamese civilians were assassinated from 1969 to 1972.

"The CIA has assassinated thousands of people.... When the history of the CIA's support of torturers gets written ... it'll be the all-time horror story."

—Philip Agee, former CIA agent, 1975.

Q: "Any assassination or assassination attempt would have to have the highest approval?"

A: "That's correct."

Q: "From the president?"

A: "That is correct."

—Richard Bissell, CIA Chief of Clandestine Services, 1959–1961. Bissell was being questioned by a commission headed by Vice President Nelson Rockefeller on the question of presidential authorization of assassinations by the CIA, 1975.

"You will recall that I mentioned that the local circumstances under which a given means might be used might suggest the technique to be used in that case. I think the gross divisions in presenting this subject might be:

I. bodies left with no hope of the cause of death being determined by the most complete autopsy and chemical examinations

2. bodies left in such circumstances as to simulate accidental death

3. bodies left in such circumstances as to simulate suicidal death

4. bodies left with residue that simulate those caused by natural diseases."

"There are two techniques which I believe should be continued since they require no special equipment besides a strong arm and the will to do such a job. These would be either to smother the victim with a pillow or to strangle him with a wide piece of cloth such as a bath towel. In such cases, there are no specific anatomic changes to indicate the cause of death."

—Statements of CIA technicians, whose names were never made public, testifying in closed sessions before the Church Committee, the U.S. Senate's panel investigating CIA abuses, in 1975.

"It was not an assassination—they just wanted him to get sick for a long time."

—CIA technician Sidney Gottlieb, 1975. Gottlieb was referring to his orders by the CIA to send a handkerchief infected with poison to Iraqi military leader Abdul Karim in 1963. Karim had not long before opened diplomatic relations with the Soviets and lifted a ban on the Communist Party in Iraq.

"Mr. Reagan realizes that a good deal of dirty work has to be done."

—General Daniel Graham (Ret.), leader of a special 1979 Reagan campaign delegation sent to Guatemala to confer with the Guatemalan dictatorship regarding its war on rebel groups in the country. Death squad activity in Guatemala increased dramatically immediately following Reagan's becoming president in January 1981.

"What they should do is declare martial law. Then you catch somebody, they go to a military court, three colonels are sitting there, you're guilty, you're shot. It works very well."

—Keith Parker, Bank of America's Vice President in Guatemala, suggesting to the incoming Reagan administration how members of the Guatemalan resistance movement should be treated, 1980.

"Why should we be worried about the death squads? They're bumping off the commies, our enemies. I'd give them more power. Hell, I'd get some cartridges if I could, and everyone else would too. . . . Why should we criticize them? The death squads—I'm for it. . . . Shit! There's no question, we can't wait 'til Reagan gets in. We hope Carter falls in the ocean real quick. . . . We all feel that he [Reagan] is our savior."

—Fred Sherwood, former president of the American Chamber of Commerce in Guatemala, September 1980.

"Attacking the civilians is the game plan. . . . Kill the sympathizers and you win the war."

—Lawrence Bailey, a former U.S. Marine who served in El Salvador as a mercenary soldier for the U.S.-sponsored Salvadoran death squads during the 1980s.

"D'Aubuisson has served as principal henchman for the wealthy landowners and as coordinator of the right-wing death squads that have murdered several thousand suspected leftists and leftist sympathizers during the past year."

—Excerpt from a March 1981 CIA report to Vice President George H. W. Bush.

"We've always had a hard time getting them to take prisoners instead of ears."

—An advisor from the U.S. Army School of Special Forces referring to
the murder of at least 1,000 peasants, mostly women and elderly, in
the Salvadoran village of El Mozote in December 1981.

"These events don't constitute assassinations because as far as we are concerned assassinations are only those of heads of state."

—Duane "Dewey" Clarridge, CIA division chief in charge of Nicaraguan paramilitary operations in the Reagan administration, 1983. Clarridge was asked in a congressional hearing about the CIA-supported Contra assassinations of health workers, teachers, and government employees in Nicaragua.

"We were made to kill dogs and vultures by biting their throats and twisting off their heads, and had to watch as soldiers tortured and killed suspect[s] . . . tearing out their fingernails, cutting off their heads, cutting a body into pieces. . . . Recruits were told that . . . torturing people and animals 'makes you more of a man and gives you more courage.'"

—A Salvadoran soldier, who in 1990 deserted from his military unit and fled to the United States, speaking of his training by U.S. Special Forces personnel during the 1980s. His name was kept secret for his own protection.

"Then they began to teach us how to torture. One evening they went and got nine young people that were accused of being guerrillas and brought them to where we were. . . . The first one they brought—a young fellow who was around 15 or 16 years old . . . was the first one that died under torture. . . . The officers said, 'We're going to teach you how to mutilate and how to teach a lesson to these guerrillas.' The officers who were teaching us this were the American Green Berets. Then they began to torture this young fellow. They took out their knives and stuck them under his fingernails. After they took his fingernails off, then they broke his elbows. Afterwards they gouged out his eyes. They took their bayonets and made all sorts of slices in his skin all around his chest, arms, and legs. They then took his hair off and the skin of his scalp. When they saw there was nothing left to do with him, they threw gasoline on him and burned him."

—Carlos Montano, former Salvadoran death squad member during the 1980s.

"I give Reagan and co. good marks, and encourage more military aid to Latin-style fascists . . . regardless of how many are murdered, because there are higher American priorities than Salvadoran human rights."

—Journalist Stacy Sullivan in an article in *The New Republic*, May 1984.

"The torture is part of the U.S. counterinsurgency program in El Salvador—with U.S. servicemen often acting as supervisors."

—Excerpt from "The Mariona Report," smuggled out of El Salvador's Mariona Prison and documenting 40 different kinds of torture being administered to political prisoners, 1986.

"The Contra forces were trained to kill communists, and this is an important thing because they might react in a situation where the only good communists are dead communists. So they kill people who they don't have to kill, women and children. Sometimes terror is very productive."

"In 1983, 1984, [the CIA] knew everything, they were monitoring all actions. They were exposed to all atrocities, abuses. I talked to the CIA, the station chief, to the deputies, of what I knew. We talked only to high people in the CIA, and those people used to say that the White House knew very well what was going on."

—Edgar Chamorro, 1986. Chamorro was a former Contra leader who worked with the Reagan administration and the CIA during the 1980s.

"We have to work, though, sort of the dark side. . . . A lot of what needs to be done here will have to be done quietly, without any discussion."

—Vice President Dick Cheney, on *Meet the Press*, September 16, 2001, setting the stage for the U.S. response called "The War on Terror." In the summer of 2006 the U.S. Supreme Court ruled that for the past five years the Bush administration's treatment of terrorist suspects had been in violation of American law, U.S. military law, and the Geneva Conventions.

"My impression is that what has been charged thus far is abuse, which I believe technically is different from torture. I don't know if it is correct to say what you just said, that torture has taken place, or that there's been a conviction for torture. And therefore I'm not going to address the torture word."

—Secretary of Defense Donald Rumsfeld, speaking before a senate committee investigating torture at the Abu Ghraib prison in Iraq, May 2004.

"This is no different than what happens at the Skull and Bones initiation, and we're going to ruin people's lives over it and we're going to hamper our military effort, and then we are going to really hammer them because they had a good time. You know, these people are being fired at every day. I'm talking about people having a good time, these people, you ever heard of emotional release? You ever heard of the need to blow some steam off? . . . You know, if you look at—if you, really, if you look at these pictures, I mean, I don't know if it's just me, but it looks like anything you'd see Madonna or Britney Spears do on stage. . . . I mean, this is something that you can see on stage at Lincoln Center from an NEA grant, maybe on *Sex in the City*, the movie."

"It's sort of like hazing, a fraternity prank. Sort of like that kind of fun."

—Rush Limbaugh, commenting on the abuse of Iraqi prisoners by U.S. military personnel at the Abu Ghraib prison in Iraq, May 3–4, 2004.

"The Christian in me says it's wrong, but the corrections officer in me says, 'I love to make a grown man piss himself.'"

—Specialist Charles Graner, Abu Ghraib prison guard, explaining his treatment of Iraqi detainees for Sergeant Joseph M. Darby, May 22, 2004.

"[A] new paradigm renders obsolete [the Geneva Conventions'] strict limitations on questioning of enemy prisoners and renders quaint some of its provisions."

—Attorney General Alberto Gonzales, when questioned about the U.S. use of torture in violation of the Geneva Conventions, 2004.

"We need to shut down this Gitmo prison? Well, don't shut it down—we just need to start an advertising campaign. We need to call it, 'Gitmo, the Muslim resort.' Any resort that treated people like this would have ads all over the *New York Times* trying to get people to come down and visit for some R&R, for some rest and relaxation."

—Rush Limbaugh, *The Rush Limbaugh Show*, June 14, 2005.

"Hugo Chavez thinks we're trying to assassinate him. I think that we really ought to go ahead and do it. . . . It is a whole lot cheaper than starting a war, and I don't think any oil shipments will stop. This is a dangerous enemy to our south controlling a huge pool of oil that could hurt us very badly. . . . We don't need another $200 billion war. . . . It's a whole lot easier to have some of the covert operatives do the job and get it over with."

—Reverend Pat Robertson, August 26, 2005.

"We must all be prepared to torture. Having established that, we can then begin to work together to codify rules of interrogation for the very unpleasant but very real cases in which we are morally permitted—indeed morally compelled—to do terrible things."

—Charles Krauthammer, *The Weekly Standard*, December 5, 2005.

"Now you can get into a debate about what shocks the conscience and what is cruel and inhuman. And to some extent, I suppose, that's in the eye of the beholder. . . . The rule is whether or not it shocks the conscience."

—Vice President Dick Cheney, during an interview on *Nightline*, December 18, 2005. Cheney had been asked where the president drew the line on torture.

"The CIA doesn't see this as a problem. . . . Uzbekistan has been a good partner in the war on terror."

—CIA station chief in Tashkent, Uzbekistan, to Craig Murray, British ambassador to Uzbekistan, when Murray brought up Uzbekistan's abysmal human rights record, including the "specialty" of their state police in handling prisoners kidnapped by the CIA and delivered to them for "questioning"—boiling them alive, February 2005.

Random Topics

"Blessed are the young, for they shall inherit the national debt."

—President Herbert Hoover, October 1930.

"Needs a bath and a haircut."

—President Harry S. Truman, in his diary, after meeting Albert Einstein, January 19, 1948.

"Any son of a bitch tries to shoot me, I'll take the gun away from him, stick it up his ass and pull the trigger."

—President Harry S. Truman, October 1949.

"You are a frustrated old man who wishes he could have been successful. Someday I hope to meet you. When that happens, you'll need a new nose, a lot of beef steak for black eyes, and perhaps a supporter below!"

—President Harry S. Truman, 1952, in a letter to *Washington Post* critic Paul Hume, who had written a column about Truman's daughter Margaret's music recital in Constitutional Hall. Hume had written: "Miss Truman cannot sing very well. She is flat a good deal of the time."

"This is why!"

—President Lyndon B. Johnson, October 1966, as he pulled his penis out of his pants and shook it at journalists who persisted in asking him why the United States was sending men to fight in Vietnam. (LBJ always referred to his penis as "Jumbo.")

"I know I am. That's my prerogative."

—President Lyndon B. Johnson, 1967, to one of his Secret Service men. Standing next to LBJ, the agent felt his leg getting wet and said to Johnson, "You're pissing on my leg, Mr. President."

"It was only a cigarette burn."

—George W. Bush, quoted in the *New York Times*, 1967. Bush was responding to an editorial in the *Yale Daily News* about his participation in the tradition of "branding" new pledges as a part of the initiation ceremonies in his Delta Kappa Epsilon fraternity while he was a junior at Yale. The initiates were often "branded" by a hot wire hanger or a lit cigarette.

"I didn't learn a damn thing at Yale."

—George W. Bush, to family members, about his years at Yale University, 1964–1968.

"I don't want our foreign policy run by the striped-pants faggots in Foggy Bottom."

—President Richard M. Nixon, commenting on his distrust of the U.S. State Department, March 1969.

"I admired Hitler, for instance, because he came from being a little man with almost no formal education up to power."

—Arnold Schwarzenegger, in a 1975 interview during the filming of the documentary *Pumping Iron*.

"People should not live in those areas. They know the problem."

—A Pentagon spokesman responding to a question about why the U.S. military refused to provide mine maps to civilian mine-deactivation teams in Indochina, in 1989. Over the years thousands of Indochinese have died as a result of exploding mines.

"This guy is mighty fucked up."

—George W. Bush, 1992, speaking to a friend about Bill Clinton defeating his father in the presidential election of 1992.

"I don't have the foggiest idea about what I think about international foreign policy."

—George W. Bush to Prince Bandar bin Sultan, Saudi Arabian ambassador to the United States, 1998.

"Do you know why Chelsea Clinton is so ugly? Because Janet Reno is her father."

—Senator John McCain, at a Republican fund-raiser, 1998.

"It was, of course, picked up and politicized. You know, 'Bush to Jews: Go to Hell!' It was very ugly. It hurt my feelings."

—George W. Bush, January 1999. Bush had earlier told a Jewish reporter that Jesus was the only way to heaven.

"Rest assured, I would not appoint somebody to a position who was an open homosexual."

—George W. Bush, speaking to a group of right-wing religious leaders called the "Madison Project," September 1999.

Andy Hiller: "Do you believe yourself to be weak on foreign policy?"

George W. Bush: "No. I've got a clear vision of where I want to lead America."

Hiller: "Can you name the president of Chechnya?"

Bush: "No, can you?"

Hiller: "Can you name the president of Taiwan?"

Bush: "Yeah. Lee. Wait a minute—is this 50 Questions?"

Hiller: "No, it's four questions of four leaders of four hot spots. The leader of Pakistan?"

Bush: "The new Pakistani general. Just been elected—he's not been elected. The guy took over office. . . . It appears he's going to bring stability to the country, and I think that's good news for the subcontinent."

Hiller: "And you can name him?"

Bush: "General—I can name the general . . . "

Hiller: "And it's . . . "

Bush: "General."

Hiller: "How about the prime minister of India?"

Bush: "Uh . . . no. Can *you* name the foreign minister of Mexico?"

Hiller: "No, sir. But I would say to that, *I'm* not running for president."

—From *7 News* in New Hampshire, November 1, 1999.

"One of the keys to being seen as a great leader is to be seen as a commander in chief. I'm going to get everything passed that I want to get passed and I'm going to have a successful presidency."

—President-elect George W. Bush, to author Mickey Herskowitz, December 2000.

"I had a drinking problem. Right now I should be in a bar, not the Oval Office."

—President George W. Bush, speaking to a group of religious leaders, February 2001.

"This is a fellow who is willing to commit youngsters to their death and he, himself, tries to hide. So I don't know where he is. You know, I just don't spend that much time on him, to be honest with you. . . . I truly am not that concerned about him."

—President George W. Bush, March 13, 2002, answering a reporter who had asked him, "Mr. President, in your speeches now you rarely talk about or mention Osama Bin Laden. Why is that?"

"History? We don't know. We'll all be dead."

—President George W. Bush to Bob Woodward, 2003. Bush was responding to the statement by Abraham Lincoln in 1862: "We cannot escape history."

"If the self-evident truths of our founding fathers are true
for us, they are true for all."

—George W. Bush, March 2003.

"The images you are seeing on TV you are seeing over, and
over, and over, and it's the same picture of some person
walking out of some building with a vase, and you see it 20
times, and you think, My goodness, were there that many
vases? [laughter] Is it possible that there were that many
ancient vases in the whole country?"

"Think what's happened in our cities when we've had riots,
and problems, and looting. Stuff happens! Freedom's
untidy. Free people are free to make mistakes and commit crimes."

—Secretary of Defense Donald Rumsfeld, in answer to questions
at press conferences, April 11-12, 2003, about the looting of
museums and ancient monuments in Iraq as the U.S. occupation
forces took over Baghdad. According to some accounts from the
Coalition Provisional Authority, an estimated $12 billion worth of
art, archaeological pieces, etc. were lost from Baghdad's National
Museum of Antiquities while U.S. troops sat idly by at the Baghdad
airport.

"I think all foreigners should stop interfering in the internal affairs of Iraq."

—Paul Wolfowitz, U.S. deputy secretary of defense, July 22, 2003.

"Every time an American soldier, sailor, or Marine risks his or her life to ensure our security and peace, Ronald Reagan will be there."

—Ken Mehlman, George W. Bush's campaign manager, speaking to the Iowa Republican Party convention, June 2004.

"I wish these assholes would put things just point-blank to me. I get half a book telling me about the history of North Korea."

—President George W. Bush, March 2005, regarding staff reports to him on the importance of North Korea.

"These broads are millionaires, lionized on TV and in articles about them, reveling in their status as celebrities and stalked by grief-arazzies. I've never seen people enjoying their husbands' deaths so much."

—Ann Coulter, speaking about activist widows of victims of 9/11, June 2006.

About the Author

Jim Hunt was born and raised in St. Helena, California, in the heart of the Napa Valley wine country. He has taught high school history and government in California public schools for over 30 years. During that time, he has researched hundreds of books relating to the secret history of the U.S. government during the Cold War. He holds a master's degree in secondary education from Tufts University. Jim is currently retired from teaching and is living in Napa, California.

Other Books from PoliPointPress

The Blue Pages: A Directory of Companies
Rated by Their Politics and Practices

Helps consumers match their buying decisions with their political values by listing the political contributions and business practices of over 1,000 companies. $9.95, PAPERBACK.

Sasha Abramsky, Breadline USA: The Hidden Scandal of American Hunger and How to Fix It

Treats the increasing food insecurity crisis in America not only as a matter of failed policies, but also as an issue of real human suffering. $23.95, CLOTH.

Rose Aguilar, Red Highways:
A Liberal's Journey into the Heartland

Challenges red state stereotypes to reveal new strategies for progressives. $15.95, PAPERBACK.

Dean Baker, Plunder and Blunder:
The Rise and Fall of the Bubble Economy

Chronicles the growth and collapse of the stock and housing bubbles and explains how policy blunders and greed led to the catastrophic—but completely predictable—market meltdowns. $15.95, PAPERBACK.

Jeff Cohen, Cable News Confidential:
My Misadventures in Corporate Media

Offers a fast-paced romp through the three major cable news channels—Fox CNN, and MSNBC—and delivers a serious message about their failure to cover the most urgent issues of the day. $14.95, PAPERBACK.

Marjorie Cohn, *Cowboy Republic:*
Six Ways the Bush Gang Has Defied the Law

Shows how the executive branch under President Bush has systematically defied the law instead of enforcing it. $14.95, PAPERBACK.

Marjorie Cohn and Kathleen Gilberd, *Rules of Disengagement:*
The Politics and Honor of Military Dissent

Examines what U.S. military men and women have done—and what their families and others can do—to resist illegal wars, as well as military racism, sexual harassment, and denial of proper medical care. $14.95, PAPERBACK.

Joe Conason, *The Raw Deal: How the Bush Republicans*
Plan to Destroy Social Security and the Legacy of the New Deal

Reveals the well-financed and determined effort to undo the Social Security Act and other New Deal programs. $11.00, PAPERBACK.

Kevin Danaher, Shannon Biggs, and Jason Mark,
Building the Green Economy: Success Stories from the
Grassroots

Shows how community groups, families, and individual citizens have protected their food and water, cleaned up their neighborhoods, and strengthened their local economies. $16.00, PAPERBACK.

Kevin Danaher and Alisa Gravitz, *The Green Festival Reader:*
Fresh Ideas from Agents of Change

Collects the best ideas and commentary from some of the most forward green thinkers of our time. $15.95, PAPERBACK.

Reese Erlich, *Dateline Havana:*
The Real Story of U.S. Policy and the Future of Cuba

Explores Cuba's strained relationship with the United States, the island nation's evolving culture and politics, and prospects for U.S. Cuba policy with the departure of Fidel Castro. $22.95, HARDCOVER.

Reese Erlich, *The Iran Agenda:*
The Real Story of U.S. Policy and the Middle East Crisis

Explores the turbulent recent history between the two countries and how it has led to a showdown over nuclear technology. $14.95, PAPERBACK.

Steven Hill, *10 Steps to Repair American Democracy*

Identifies the key problems with American democracy, especially election practices, and proposes ten specific reforms to reinvigorate it. $11.00, PAPERBACK.

Markos Kounalakis and Peter Laufer, *Hope Is a Tattered Flag:*
Voices of Reason and Change for the Post-Bush Era

Gathers together the most listened-to politicos and pundits, activists and thinkers, to answer the question: what happens after Bush leaves office? $29.95, HARDCOVER; $16.95 PAPERBACK.

Yvonne Latty, *In Conflict: Iraq War Veterans*
Speak Out on Duty, Loss, and the Fight to Stay Alive

Features the unheard voices, extraordinary experiences, and personal photographs of a broad mix of Iraq War veterans, including Congressman Patrick Murphy, Tammy Duckworth, Kelly Daugherty, and Camilo Mejia. $24.00, HARDCOVER.

Phillip Longman, *Best Care Anywhere:*
Why VA Health Care Is Better Than Yours

Shows how the turnaround at the long-maligned VA hospitals provides a blueprint for salvaging America's expensive but troubled health care system. $14.95, PAPERBACK.

Phillip Longman and Ray Boshara, *The Next Progressive Era*

Provides a blueprint for a re-empowered progressive movement and describes its implications for families, work, health, food, and savings. $22.95, HARDCOVER.

Marcia and Thomas Mitchell, *The Spy Who Tried to Stop a War: Katharine Gun and the Secret Plot to Sanction the Iraq Invasion*

Describes a covert operation to secure UN authorization for the Iraq war and the furor that erupted when a young British spy leaked it. $23.95, HARDCOVER.

Susan Mulcahy, ed., *Why I'm a Democrat*

Explores the values and passions that make a diverse group of Americans proud to be Democrats. $14.95, PAPERBACK.

David Neiwert, *The Eliminationists: How Hate Talk Radicalized the American Right*

Argues that the conservative movement's alliances with far-right extremists have not only pushed the movement's agenda to the right, but also have become a malignant influence increasingly reflected in political discourse. $16.95, PAPERBACK.

Christine Pelosi, *Campaign Boot Camp: Basic Training for Future Leaders*

Offers a seven-step guide for successful campaigns and causes at all levels of government. $15.95, PAPERBACK.

William Rivers Pitt, *House of Ill Repute: Reflections on War, Lies, and America's Ravaged Reputation*

Skewers the Bush Administration for its reckless invasions, warrantless wiretaps, lethally incompetent response to Hurricane Katrina, and other scandals and blunders. $16.00, PAPERBACK.

Sarah Posner, *God's Profits:*
Faith, Fraud, and the Republican Crusade for Values Voters

Examines corrupt televangelists' ties to the Republican Party and unprecedented access to the Bush White House. $19.95, HARDCOVER.

Nomi Prins, *Jacked: How "Conservatives" Are Picking Your Pocket-Whether You Voted for Them or Not*

Describes how the "conservative" agenda has affected your wallet, skewed national priorities, and diminished America—but not the American spirit. $12.00, PAPERBACK.

Cliff Schecter, *The Real McCain: Why Conservatives Don't Trust Him—And Why Independents Shouldn't*

Explores the gap between the public persona of John McCain and the reality of this would-be president. $14.95, HARDCOVER.

Norman Solomon, *Made Love, Got War:*
Close Encounters with America's Warfare State

Traces five decades of American militarism and the media's all-too-frequent failure to challenge it. $24.95, HARDCOVER.

John Sperling et al., *The Great Divide: Retro vs. Metro America*

Explains how and why our nation is so bitterly divided into what the authors call Retro and Metro America. $19.95, PAPERBACK.

Daniel Weintraub, *Party of One:*
Arnold Schwarzenegger and the Rise of the Independent Voter

Explains how Schwarzenegger found favor with independent voters, whose support has been critical to his success, and suggests that his bipartisan approach represents the future of American politics. $19.95, HARDCOVER.

Curtis White,
The Barbaric Heart: Faith, Money, and the Crisis of Nature

Argues that the solution to the present environmental crisis may come from an unexpected quarter: the arts, religion, and the realm of the moral imagination. $16.95, PAPERBACK.

Curtis White,
The Spirit of Disobedience: Resisting the Charms of Fake Politics, Mindless Consumption, and the Culture of Total Work

Debunks the notion that liberalism has no need for spirituality and describes a "middle way" through our red state/blue state political impasse. Includes three powerful interviews with John DeGraaf, James Howard Kunstler, and Michael Ableman. $24.00, HARDCOVER.

For more information, please visit www.p3books.com.

About This Book

This book is printed on Cascade Enviro100 Print paper. It contains 100 percent post-consumer fiber and is certified EcoLogo, Processed Chlorine Free, and FSC Recycled. For each ton used instead of virgin paper, we:

- Save the equivalent of 17 trees
- Reduce air emissions by 2,098 pounds
- Reduce solid waste by 1,081 pounds
- Reduce the water used by 10,196 gallons
- Reduce suspended particles in the water by 6.9 pounds.

This paper is manufactured using biogas energy, reducing natural gas consumption by 2,748 cubic feet per ton of paper produced.

The book's printer, Malloy Incorporated, works with paper mills that are environmentally responsible, that do not source fiber from endangered forests, and that are third-party certified. Malloy prints with soy and vegetable based inks, and over 98 percent of the solid material they discard is recycled. Their water emissions are entirely safe for disposal into their municipal sanitary sewer system, and they work with the Michigan Department of Environmental Quality to ensure that their air emissions meet all environmental standards.

The Michigan Department of Environmental Quality has recognized Malloy as a Great Printer for their compliance with environmental regulations, written environmental policy, pollution prevention efforts, and pledge to share best practices with other printers. Their county Department of Planning and Environment has designated them a Waste Knot Partner for their waste prevention and recycling programs.